MR. RIGHT

AND

MY LEFT KIDNEY

MR. RIGHT and MY LEFT KIDNEY

Joan Saltzman

Peripety Press
Philadelphia

www.peripetypress.com

Published by Peripety Press, Philadelphia

Library of Congress Control Number: 2006933615

ISBN-13: 978-0-9789521-7-4

ISBN-10: 0-9789521-7-0

10 9 8 7 6 5 4 3 2 1

To John Stuart Katz,
without whom none of this would have been possible

Acknowledgments

I am indebted to the strangers who spurred me on by saying, "It is the most romantic story I ever heard. I can't wait to read it." I am grateful to my oldest (not in years but in longevity) friend, Jeannie Friedman, who kept telling me "You can do it," at times when I lost my nerve, and who helped me every step of the way with her keen eye and warm heart, and to Billie Schnall for her unwavering friendship and support. Thanks too to my editor and friend, Bonnie Clause, for her fastidious attention to the text and her respect for my voice, and to Kelly Blair, who gave this book its shape, for her fertile imagination and her divine patience.

But most of all, I am grateful to John Stuart Katz for providing me with a great love story, boundless encouragement and the generosity to let me tell our story my way.

LATE BLOOMER

The word as I approached my forty-sixth birthday was that I, now well over forty, had as much chance of getting married as being killed by an Albanian terrorist. I'm not making this up. It supposedly came from some Yale study. That prediction is now neither statistically nor politically correct. By forty-five I had given up on the idea that there was still time to meet Mr. Right, settle down and have Baby Rights. Although there were stories of women having babies in their fifties, even up to sixty, I couldn't imagine handling a cranky teenager while cashing Social Security checks. I hadn't given up on finding a husband but I had at last put the quest on a back burner.

I had always been a late bloomer. Blooming late had been a family trait. My parents, Rose and Sam, met and married when they were both thirty-five, an advanced age for marriage in 1946. I had been convinced to save myself for marriage and by the time I realized at twenty-two that no proposal was in the offing, and that saving myself for anything in the sex, drugs and rock and roll sixties was pure folly, I was the last of my girlfriends to lose her virginity.

I had more than my share of Mr. Wrongs. Any single woman over twenty will recognize the types—narcissistic, psychotic, married, cheap, gay, bisexual, the professor, the student, the boss, the alcoholic, the drug addict, the chauvinist, the stalker, the commitment-phobic, the man who doesn't listen to a word you say, the guy who is always right, the fellow who hates his ex-wife, his kids and/or his mother, the man who can't make up his mind about anything, including whether to order the linguine or the angel hair, and some who were a combination of two or three of the above.

I would be lying if I said my inability to find Mr. Right by my forties was everyone else's fault. I had certainly run across my share of nice, caring guys, but I invariably found them wanting.

Although my Mr. Right eluded me, I had no intention of settling, even though everyone encouraged me to do just that. My mother, who was growing increasingly desperate to have grandchildren, said on my thirtieth birthday, "You're setting your sights too high. Do you think that Prince Charming will ride up to your house on a white horse and knock on the door?" By my fortieth birthday she said, "Joan, you're never going to find the perfect guy. Just find someone, anyone, so you won't be alone for the rest of your life." My women friends rarely said anything. They just looked at me compassionately when I told them one more tale about my love life. My male friends increasingly suggested that I should be more realistic and just give one of these guys a chance, even if he wasn't exactly what I had my heart set on.

I didn't see much reason to settle on the wrong guy. I had always had an optimistic streak. I just figured if I waited long enough the right person would come along. I didn't really need a man. I could support myself. I was a lawyer. I owned my own house. I had wonderful, caring friends. I did yearn for the companionship of someone who shared my dreams and my interests, and I thought that some day the right guy would knock on my door. Maybe not literally. Maybe he wouldn't be on a white horse. The horse I could do without. To tell the truth, once I got a few years into my forties I began to wonder if I should lower my expectations and just be happy with the next guy who came along no matter how flawed he was and how little we had in common. I didn't do that though, and, boy, am I happy I didn't.

JUST LIKE IN THE MOVIES

In August of 1993, at almost forty-six, I hadn't yet come up with the right formula for meeting the prince I had been promised in fairy tales and Disney movies, when suddenly the planets or something converged or diverged and everything seemed to fall into place. The tide began to turn in my favor during a trip to the Montreal World Film Festival. I had been a film buff since seeing my first Martin and Lewis movie with my dad on the Atlantic City Boardwalk when I was four. I decided to try following the conventional self-help wisdom at the time—"If you do what you love, you'll find someone whose interests are compatible." I went to the festival with my friends Ruth and Archie Perlmutter, film teachers and movie festival aficionados who married in 1947, the year I was born, and who were still going strong when we went to Montreal together, fueled by an intense mutual love of movies.

Once I passed my mid-forties and my biological clock had ticked out, I was no longer so determined to find Mr. Right. My mother had died a few years before the Montreal trip, lessening the incessant pressure to "Find a guy. Get married." If it happened, fine. If not, I had no complaints. With all of the pressure to find my soul mate finally off, I was more relaxed and less needy. When I was feeling needy it was as if I had a neon sign on my chest that blinked a scarlet "N" in bright red letters. Now the sign was flickering only now and then. I was also more open to Mr. Almost Right. I had finally figured out that there were no perfect people, let alone perfect available guys. If Mr. Even Almost Right were around the corner in Montreal, the chances of my finding him and our being able to tolerate each other were greater, in spite of the Yale study, than they had ever been before.

Over my forty plus years of being single, I had trained myself to be vigilant for any eligible looking guy who passed by. The reflex was automatic by now. On the day I arrived at the festival, I spied a man with salt-and-pepper hair and beard in the Meridien Hotel lobby. Medium height. Medium weight. That and the beard made him indistinguishable from hundreds of other cinephiles who had descended on Montreal. But, oh, his eyes. They were a striking blue-gray. On the second day of the festival I noticed the same interesting-looking man with the beautiful blue eyes that I had seen the day before. This time he was sitting on the arm of a chair. I thought better than to pursue what could at best be a short film festival fling.

The festival was winding down. I was scheduled to leave Montreal the next day. Ruth, Archie and I decided to catch a tribute to Roger Moore, an early James Bond. It was the first time during the festival that we all went to an event together. The tribute was held in the largest venue in the Place des Arts. The auditorium held thousands. We sat through many clips of an engaging and much younger Moore helping buxom damsels in distress evade various Russian-accented villains, and then helping himself to the scantily clad damsels. After the film, the very dapper, nipped-and-tucked Moore graciously accepted the accolades heaped upon him. He was jovial. The ceremony had a joyous, celebratory tone. As I clapped, cheered and laughed, I happened to turn around and several rows behind me and to the left, I saw the same guy I had seen twice in the Meridien lobby. Just a coincidence, I thought.

In contrast to the mood of the Moore tribute was the somber tone of the Italian language movie that followed, *Jonah Who Lived in the Whale,* an achingly sad tale of a four-year-old Jewish boy, his parents and the Italian Fascists, who were about to turn the family's life upside down. As with many of the films at Montreal's Festival, this movie was subtitled only in French. Here was a test of my high school French teacher's acumen.

Miss Fugate taught me French for three of my four years in high school with a combination of immersion and terrorism. We were not permitted to say one word of English in class, and by the end of the first semester my cronies and I were translating rock and roll songs into French.

Mademoiselle Fugate was not content to be compelling simply because she was a brilliant teacher. She captured our attention with fear as well. Like the time my best friend Jeanne and I had a study hall in her class. We were chewing gum. "I smell chewing gum," she announced in a kind of cackle that reminded me of the wicked witch in *The Wizard of Oz* when the witch said to Dorothy, "And your little dog, too."

"Oh no," we said, almost in unison.

"Yes, you are and I am going to put it on your permanent records and no college will ever accept you."

I was crushed. My life was over. I saw college as my only hope for the future since I had wanted to be a lawyer ever since I saw my hero Perry Mason win every case on TV. I couldn't type and never did well in sewing or cooking classes. Tearfully I came home and broke the bad news to my mother, "I'm not going to college."

"What do you mean? What happened?"

"I got caught chewing gum and now it's on my permanent record."

I still don't know how she kept from laughing.

Could I read the subtitles and make any sense out of the Italian movie? I could. Miss Fugate, wherever you are, fear does work as a pedagogical tool. I felt so cultured, so cosmopolitan— an Italian movie in Montreal with French subtitles—and I could understand it. It helped that the main character was four years old and was speaking nursery school Italian, which was then translated into nursery school French at the bottom of the screen.

My companions and I left the Place des Arts with the herds of others who had attended the tribute and film. We stood on the street corner talking about the movie, when suddenly I saw the guy with the bewitching blue eyes. Ruth was waving at him. "John," she called. He was walking over. As he got closer I realized that he was even better looking than I thought. He was five foot eight, late forties I guessed, and, oh, those eyes.

We all stood on the corner talking but Ruth and Archie faded away just like when Rossano Brazzi sings "Some Enchanted Evening" in the movie *South Pacific* and all that he sees is Mitzi Gaynor. Suddenly it was just the bearded blue-eyed guy and me. Ruth introduced him—"John Katz." He was even Jewish. Wouldn't my mother have been happy? He was a professor at a university in Toronto and had his doctorate from Harvard. The Harvard part appealed to me. He taught film. My passion. Married? I didn't know. No ring. He proudly talked about his son, Jesse, who had settled on college in Montreal after a year of following the Grateful Dead. John and Jesse were visiting the hot spot Montreal delis for smoked meat sandwiches and fries with curds, he said. I was puzzled by that. My only association with curds had been Little Bo Peep and she had them with whey.

The woman John saw when we met on that street corner was finally coming into her own. I had shed the baby fat that had been plaguing me for years and settled into a size 6. My naturally curly brunette hair was in vogue. My eyes were large and brown, my smile warm and broad. That day the scarlet "N" was nowhere in sight.

John and I talked while I was in my magical haze for what seemed like a long time. He was charming and engaging. He thought it was great that I was a lawyer. Plenty of men had been put off by my profession. He told a slew of jokes, although I can't remember one of them. I laughed a lot. He gave me his card. I didn't have one. "Simon and Garfunkel are coming to New York soon, a comeback tour," John said.

"I'd love to see them. I know all their songs," I replied.

Lucky for me he said Simon and Garfunkel and not Alice Cooper, Kiss or, God forbid, Led Zeppelin. I really did know every song Simon and Garfunkel ever sang. I even knew the songs from their first album, "Wednesday Morning, 3 AM." I had the annoying habit in the early Simon and Garfunkel days of playing their records again and again until I knew all of the words. I lost college roommates over that. I meant it when I said I would love to see one of their rare reunion concerts.

Well, we said goodnight, and I could have kicked myself because I didn't suggest that we do something right then and there, or at least make a definite plan to see Simon and Garfunkel.

I knew I would be greeted when I returned home from Montreal, not by a loving family like in the *Father Knows Best* and *Donna Reed* TV shows I grew up with, but by the typical family of the single woman in urban America—my orange tabbies, Mickey and Sally.

I unlocked the door. Mickey and Sally ran to greet me.

THE GIRL WITH THE HAT

When I arrived home from Montreal, I decided to investigate one Professor John Katz. I was a lawyer, after all, and trained to investigate. I started with Ruth.

"So what do you know about him?"

"He's a little neurotic and he has a girlfriend, I think. Every time I see her she's wearing a hat."

"A hat? What else?"

"She looks Russian."

Aha. So this was my competition, the Russian girl with the hat. Mr. Seemingly Right was morphing into Mr. Apparently Not So Good. My usual reaction would have been to write this guy off. I could never stand competition. I never thought I could win. My defeatist attitude was exacerbated in junior high when the popular girls convinced me I could never measure up. Well, I wasn't in junior high any more and that attitude never got me anywhere.

I quizzed Ruth more. I didn't bother to ask her about the neurotic part. Far be it from me, a recovering hypochondriac and neurotic myself, to reject someone because of neurosis. I had never met an interesting person who wasn't at least slightly neurotic. Ruth knew little more about The Girl with the Hat except that she lived in Canada. Ruth hadn't talked to The Girl much except to exchange pleasantries, so all we knew about her was superficial.

The hat as a distinguishing feature was useful to me because there was something very unlike me about it. Had I been thinking more clearly I would have realized that there must have been things about the woman (or the hat) that John liked or he would have tossed the girl and the hat out on their ears.

I had never been someone who could wear a hat. My mounds of dark curls prevented it. Whenever I thought it might be a good idea to get a hat to protect me from the sun or cold, I would venture out to a store to try some on. Then I would hear my mother's voice saying, "That's how people get head lice." On those rare days when I decided to brave the lice, I'd try on hats one after the other. Invariably each was too small to make its way over my mane and each would sit precariously on top of my head, a little like the tiny hats clowns wear perched on their red wooly wigs. And so, if anyone who knew me described me, I would always be the hatless one, the girl without the hat.

I was determined this time I was going to try a different strategy. I was going to compete, like I did in the courtroom, and win. I would win John's heart and The Girl with the Hat would be vanquished, banished to the corner of a film festival party, her hat knocked unceremoniously off her head.

world series miracle

I waited a few days after I talked to Ruth to call John, hoping, as
even the most modern of women does, that he would call me first.
After the first few awkward seconds when I reminded him who I
was, he said (in the time-honored way most men would have
responded), "I was just about to call you."

Meanwhile the underdog Philadelphia Phillies were battling
it out with the Atlanta Braves for the National League
Championship. The Toronto Blue Jays had already clinched the
American League World Series berth. Another underdog in
Philadelphia was vying for the attention of a certain film profes-
sor in Toronto. No one thought that the Phillies could pull it out.
Same for the woman who in 1993 had as much chance of getting
the professor's long-range attention as being whacked by an
Albanian terrorist. I sent John a Phillies cap after the first time
we spoke to let him know I was still interested. And the Phillies

pulled it off. A real long shot. The Phillies were poised on the edge of a World Series with Toronto, a team that played most of their games indoors. If the scrappy Phillies could beat anyone it would be this cowardly team that was so afraid of getting cold and wet in the summer that they needed a dome to protect them.

John made me believe that he knew more about baseball than he really did. I made him think that I knew less. It was the first time I heeded my mother's often-repeated advice to "not let a man know how smart I was right off the bat."

Once when we were talking on the phone, John told me that he had met Sandy Koufax in his Ohio hometown at his Aunt Elsie's Passover seder. Koufax apparently had something to do with the University of Cincinnati then. When he played for the Brooklyn Dodgers, Sandy Koufax was one of my father's heroes. He was one of the few Jewish baseball players, and he wasn't shy about taking off on *Rosh Hashanah* and *Yom Kippur,* a way of announcing, "Say it loud. I'm Jewish and I'm proud." And then he pitched a perfect game—no hits, no runs, no walks, nine innings, twenty-seven players at bat, twenty-seven outs.

I came to the love of baseball and the Phillies honestly, being the only child of a father who loved the game. One of the Phillies catchers, Clay Dalrymple, lived across the street from the house where I grew up. My dad had only short blocks of time off from his rigorous work schedule in the mom-and-pop drugstore my parents owned. Sam had graduated first in his class in pharmacy school on the cusp of the Depression. Because there were no jobs for fledgling druggists, my father got a job in a liquor store. When he met my mother, she decided he should go back to being a professional man. Soon after they married they bought a pharmacy in Oxford Circle, one of the new row house neighborhoods that sprang up in Philadelphia after World War II.

My dad and I did two things together—played catch and watched baseball on TV. My father and I would stretch out on the floor in the living room starting when I was about four. Sometimes I would lie on my stomach, my head propped up with my hands, just inches away from the TV. That was in the days when there were no warnings about being irradiated by sitting too close. I don't think that I understood the game too well when I first starting watching, but it was always a way to spend uninterrupted time with my father. He explained the game to me. I listened and learned. He was proud that I was such a good student, both of baseball and everything else. He gloried in my academic achievements. He didn't care, as my mother did, if my clothes were askew or my bushy hair was out of place. I inherited my dad's empathy and kindness, although I never delivered a prescription to a sick child in the middle of the night as he did. We both ignored my mother's warnings that it wasn't good to be too nice because people would take advantage.

Although my mother wasn't thrilled about it, I had my own baseball glove when I was small, well before the days when girls were allowed to play Little League. While my friends were playing with Ginny dolls, I was playing baseball with the boys at school. They nicknamed me "Slugger Saltzman," which was laudatory and demeaning—laudatory because it acknowledged my hitting prowess, and demeaning because smacking a baseball out of the schoolyard was not a ladylike thing to do. I did "throw like a girl," so my fielding left something to be desired. Before I was eleven I gave up playing baseball. There was just too much peer pressure to stop being a tomboy.

One day when I was eight my father got tickets to a Phillies game. By that time I already knew the names of the players, pitchers Robin Roberts and Curt Simmons, infielders Richie "Whitey" Ashburn, Eddie Bouché and Willie Jones and the catcher Stan "Lop Lop" Lopata. My favorite was an outfielder, Harry "the Horse" Anderson. I think I liked Harry best because of his nickname, or maybe because he was tall, dark and handsome. My dad decided that we would take a bus to Connie Mack Stadium or, to be more accurate, an elevated train and two buses. It seemed to me that it took forever to get there. "Are we there yet? Are we there yet?" I remember asking.

"We'll be there soon, Joanie," Sam said as he smiled at me.

My dad had a serene, slightly crooked smile and small deep-set brown eyes. His hair was already gray and he was almost bald, although he was only in his early forties. He was no fashion plate, no matter how much my mother tried to dress him up. My father never cared how he looked on the outside. At least he no longer sported the white socks he wore when Rose met him on the Boardwalk in Atlantic City. My friends always loved him. They could feel his warmth. I felt very small on those trains and buses packed with people, but also very secure in knowing that my father would never let go of my hand. He never did let go. He held my right hand tightly, leaving my left hand free for my baseball glove.

And then we arrived. Connie Mack was one of those ancient ballparks made of wood with posts everywhere. Most seats had obstructed views but no one seemed to care. It was a beautiful spring Sunday. A doubleheader. "I don't know whether my little girl will be able to make it through both games," my father said to the man who took our tickets.

When I saw the stadium for the first time I fell in love. The grass smelled freshly mowed. The sky was clear. The sun was shining. The smell of hotdogs and hot peanuts was in the air. My father was right next to me. Every time I see a baseball game I have a warm protected feeling as if my dad is still at my side. If there's a heaven and if the souls who go there have a choice of where they can hang out, I'm sure my dad is haunting a baseball stadium, although Wrigley Field is the only one left that he would really like.

On that spring day in 1956 not only was I looking forward to seeing my first live game, which alone would have been enough, but also I had a chance to see my Uncle Eddie, my dad's brother. We didn't see much of him because my mother decided that we would be closer to her side of the family. I think she thought her side was classier than my father's. Uncle Eddie had the same sweet temperament as my dad. He was a lot heavier, though, and when he hugged you, you knew you were hugged. And Uncle Eddie had the most wonderful sideline. He was a vendor at Connie Mack. Whenever he visited our house, he would bring me triangular baseball pennants. I had pennants for each of the teams hung in my basement playroom—American League on one side, National League on the other. My mother complained that they were dust collectors. Lucky for her the expansion teams didn't come along until much later. For my eighth birthday Uncle Eddie gave me an autographed baseball with the signatures of all of the Phillies—Whitey, Lop Lop and Harry the Horse were all there. I treasured that ball. My idols had each touched it.

When we got to the baseball park, there was my uncle. I had never been so proud of anyone in my family. He was standing beside a huge board filled with hundreds of Phillies souvenirs. There was also a can next to the board chock full of pennants. I ran towards him. He gave me one of his special hugs and told me, "Pick anything you want," pointing to the board. I thought for a long time. Would it be a pencil with a tiny pennant or a large round pin with Harry the Horse's face on it? And then I saw it, a tiny teddy bear dressed in a Phillies outfit. I looked at my uncle, smiled and pointed to the bear. "It's all yours, Joanie dear," my uncle Eddie beamed.

I don't remember who the Phillies played that day. I don't remember who won. My father showed me how to keep score. I cheered every time Harry the Horse made a catch. I jumped up and down whenever a Phillie got a hit. What a sound. Nothing in all of the years I watched baseball on TV prepared me for the live crack of the bat hitting the ball.

We left the ballpark five hours, four hotdogs, a bag of peanuts, two ice creams and eighteen innings later. I took my little bear to show and tell and gushed about the Phillies, my dad and my Uncle Eddie, the man with the warmest hug and the best job in the world.

My dad's schedule didn't allow for many of these excursions, but we had a few over the years. Connie Mack Stadium went the way of most of the wooden stadiums with obstructed views, replaced by the 1960s generation of all-plastic, personality-less parks. Now that generation of plastic fields is being replaced by glossy new replicas of the original wooden stadiums.

My dad and I continued to watch baseball, lying on the floor in front of the TV, until I was thirteen. Then hanging out with parents and watching baseball were frowned upon by my friends. As between my pals and my parents, even my father, there was no contest.

When I was fifteen I heard that a friend of Uncle Eddie's daughter Linda married Ruben Amaro, a Phillie. My parents talked about the match in hushed tones around me. A nice Jewish girl was marrying a Hispanic baseball player. I wondered whether Linda's friend's family was sitting *shiva* for her, the gathering held for several days after a funeral, where guests pay calls on the bereaved, even though she was very much alive. Sometimes Jewish families did that in those days, even ones that weren't Orthodox, when a son or daughter married out of the faith. I thought Linda's friend was the luckiest girl in the world. She was doing what I had only dreamed of—she was marrying a Phillie.

The Philadelphia Athletics, the local American League team, moved away, first to Kansas City and then to Oakland. My Uncle Eddie died of complications from diabetes after multiple amputations. The Phillies stayed and figured prominently in another relationship in my life.

In 1993 Phillies World Series fever gripped Philadelphia, a town known for its fickle fans. When the Phillies are on top their mascot's name is apt: The Phanatic. Now the fans were in a frenzy. The city was all decked out in Phillies' colors, red and white. Even William Penn, the bronze statue atop City Hall, who some say appears from a certain angle to be peeing on the city, had a huge Phillies cap on his head. There were Phillies pep rallies everywhere. The fans were excited in Toronto too, cozy in their dome, but less noisy.

The rivalry was on. Philadelphia vs. Toronto. Cheese steaks vs. white bread. The Phillies against the Blue Jays. John and my phone calls intensified. What started out as conversations every few days turned into daily calls. We stayed on the phone throughout the games, sometimes for hours at a time. I found out during those marathon phone calls that John had a rare quality. He actually listened to what I said.

I found out more about John during those talks. He was an only child too. He had had a difficult childhood. His father was a traveling salesman who left home for six weeks at a time, leaving John to care for his mother, who suffered from psoriasis and self-medicated with uppers and downers. As a little boy he would find his mother passed out on the bathroom floor and would help her back to bed. When John was fourteen his dad took his mother on the road, leaving John home alone to fend for himself.

Where was The Girl with the Hat? She never seemed to be at John's house. I talked to him every night. Maybe she had been a figment of Ruth's imagination.

John and I got to know each other through the heartbreaking Phillies' defeats and the Blue Jays' triumphs. The Phillies pulled out a couple of games, but the Blue Jays routed them. Unlike the last time the Phillies won the series in 1980, they didn't have a relief-pitching ace like Tug McGraw. Tug would pound his heart each time he saved a game. Our hope for a closer in 1993 was Mitch Williams, who managed to lose every game he came in to save. The Phillies' loss was disheartening to me, especially when John called after the Blue Jays clinched the Series. He and his friends were going out to celebrate. Was The Girl with the Hat going too, wearing her Blue Jays cap this time? My friends and I were in mourning, short term though it was, until another hopeful sports season began.

After the Phillies' loss neither the Flyers nor the Eagles wanted their helmets propped on William Penn's head. The bronze statue with a Phillies cap had really pissed on the city this time.

In terms of my relationship with John, the baseball season had worked out for the best. The Phillies beat the Braves, were in the World Series, and were hammered by the Blue Jays. As my mother used to tell me when I went bowling or played Monopoly with boys, "Let them win." Well, I didn't let the Blue Jays win but it didn't hurt that they did. I remain eternally grateful to the Phillies for all they have given me over the years, and for getting to the 1993 World Series and losing.

By the time the Series wound down, John and I had plans to meet in Manhattan for the Halloween weekend Simon and Garfunkel concert.

PUMPKIN IN THE BIG APPLE
or STILL CRAZY AFTER ALL THESE YEARS

My mother always taught me to write thank-you notes even before the gift was out of the box and to keep a full refrigerator to ply guests with refreshments. I'm not sure she had in mind a refrigerator in a Manhattan hotel room in preparation for a tryst.

I was prepared for Halloween weekend in New York with John. I brought the requisite candy corn, marshmallow pumpkins and chocolate witch's hats. Not to be taken for unsophisticated, I also bought wine and cheese. I was ready, I thought, for any eventuality.

I knew when John was arriving in New York. I came to the hotel hours earlier and strolled around the city buying even more snacks. By the time John got to the hotel I had enough to last until Thanksgiving in case of a Nor'easter. In the house I grew up in it was never just Ritz crackers and American cheese. There could never be enough food when company came.

I had my wardrobe all planned too. I would greet John in skintight rust colored suede pants and a black sweater. I miscalculated. John arrived earlier than I had planned and saw me in the dowdy flowered skirt and turtleneck I'd worn on the train. John didn't seem to notice or care. He was more like my dad, I decided, less concerned with appearances than what was underneath.

"I'm so glad to see you," he said as he hugged me.

"Me too." He took my hand and we went up to our room.

When we were making our plans for New York, I demurely suggested that we get a suite that had a bedroom and a living room with a pullout couch in case things were rocky. Luckily, the then not-too-pricey Esplanade Hotel, now a senior citizen residence, had a suite. By the end of October John and I had talked for weeks. We knew a lot about each other. The chemistry could go either way, although it seemed to me to be going in the right direction. A suite offered the best defense against bad breath, body odor or just plain physical incompatibility.

John unlocked the door. It was early afternoon. He liked the spread. Not the bedspread. The food spread. We settled on the couch and had a glass of wine. This was particularly odd since neither of us drank much. We adjourned quickly to the bedroom not so much because of pure lust but just to get the first sexual encounter over with so we wouldn't have the "Will we, won't we, or when will we?" hanging over our heads.

Afterward, when if either of us smoked we would be lighting a cigarette, John told me he had some confessions to make. I had been through this with men before and the confessions included things like, "I've never been able to have a relationship with anyone, not even my hamster," "I did stop beating my wife just before we got divorced" and "I think I might be gay." So I braced myself.

One of the confessions involved The Girl with the Hat. I acted surprised even though I'd known about her from the beginning. It went something like this: "I'm involved with someone but the relationship is basically over." I guess that no one has ever said in this kind of situation, "I'm involved with someone and I love her passionately. I just want to mess around with you on the side." I asked all the requisite questions about The Girl with the Hat, told him I could handle it, even though I wasn't 100 percent sure that I could, and we moved on.

There was something else, something I wasn't prepared for but afterwards thought it could be in the repertoire quite a bit if I was going to date older men. Although I had pegged John as being in his late forties when we first met, he was actually in his mid-fifties. "I have serious kidney disease," John said somberly. I was no amateur at diseases, having been a bona fide hypochondriac in my younger years and then spending the last few years sublimating my impulse to have a stunning variety of illnesses by practicing medical malpractice law, where I focused on my clients' medical conditions rather than my own. John hadn't said "kidney disease" to some medical novice. I knew a little about many ailments and much more about the ones my lawsuits involved. Since my cases up until then had involved brain damage, tattoo removal, heart surgery and trigeminal neuralgia, my knowledge about kidney disease fell into the dilettante category. I knew where I could find out about the disease John had, and made a mental note to venture off to Jefferson Hospital's library when I got home to do some intensive research.

Although either one of John's confessions would have sent someone more faint of heart than I heading for the hills, I stayed. I thought that The Girl with the Hat could be overcome. Something about the hat, I think. The kidney disease didn't seem like a big deal. John seemed fine. He looked fine too. He had lovely olive skin that made him look like he had a permanent tan, and ruddy cheeks. He said he was fatigued a lot. He was careful about how much protein he ate. Since the kidneys metabolize protein, the less protein he ate, the less went through the kidneys and the less the kidneys were stressed. I shouldn't have bothered to buy all of those cheeses at Zabar's. I had this naïve feeling that everything would be okay. It wasn't heart disease or cancer, after all. I was a malpractice lawyer when what John really needed was a kidney specialist.

The disease was discovered in John when he was in his thirties and the doctors couldn't get his blood pressure under control. The doctors stroked their chins, shook their heads and mumbled, "You are so young to have high blood pressure." They finally had the presence of mind to test his kidneys and soon after figured out that had been the problem all along.

"Nothing can be done," John told me. He was close to tears.

He just had to be careful not to eat too much protein and wait for "the other shoe to drop"—dialysis, or if he was very lucky, a transplant. Ever the optimist and always the amateur doctor, I couldn't believe that nothing could be done. Maybe I could find a miracle cure in the medical literature.

There was no doubt that I enjoyed trying to save people. I had spent five years as a public defender reasoning that poor people deserved as good a defense as the rich. I was convinced that I could save a whole segment of the population from rotting in prison. Only a naïve twenty-five year old, who saw things in stark shades of black and white, couldn't see the other side of the story. My reasoning went something like this. The people I represented hadn't had a chance, because of poor economic status and a lousy education, to make anything of themselves. They were condemned to a life of crime because of bad luck of the draw. They had grown up in the slums of North or West Philadelphia. Giving them a "get out of jail free" card was evening the score, a kind of payback for rotten luck. It took me a few years to realize that my theory was missing an important part of the equation. Looking back, it is amazing to me what I had left out: the victims. My clients were preying on their own neighbors, the people who had managed to parlay a rotten education into a decent job that kept them and their families afloat. I eventually realized that I wasn't really helping anyone. Whenever a guilty person went free he often went back home to victimize neighbors who had eked out a living in spite of the odds.

So ended my first shot at altruism. My second try was more productive. I was older then and realized that there were downsides to what I was doing. I saw no harm in keeping doctors honest by suing them when they made mistakes that hurt my clients. Victories that other lawyers and I had in those cases had some impact on the financial viability of the health care system, but probably not as much as the powers-that-be would have you believe.

I decided I would be happy to take on John as yet another salvation project. I didn't believe that there were diseases, except maybe the worst cancers, that didn't have a cure. I was sure that all I had to do was a little research and I could tell John where to go to get help.

Then John asked me the question I hated, "Why haven't you ever been married?"

"Just never found the right guy," was my glib answer.

So after a few hours in bed and the confessional time, our conversation became more mundane and we got dressed. I had at last squeezed into my suede pants and we went out to look for a Chinese restaurant on Columbus Avenue. As we were walking down the street holding hands I had the "I feel brand new" and "just like a natural woman" feeling, that post-first-time–sex-with-a-new-guy-you're-smitten-with kind of emotion.

We found a restaurant John knew and because it was only 5:00 p.m., the time a lot of Manhattanites have just finished lunch, we got right in. For the first time, I saw what John's diet was all about. He was pretty much stuck with vegetables. Not the vegetarian menu because most of that had tofu, which is chock full of protein. It was sad to see someone, especially someone who professed to love food, condemned to eat just a few vegetables. It was the first obvious sign of John's illness. He had to deny himself foods he really liked. And the vegetables would not be a cure. They might postpone the ultimate result of the disease, complete kidney failure, for a few months or years. "Some doctors," John told me, "don't believe the diet has any effect on the disease's outcome." He could have been denying himself Kung Pao Chicken and spareribs for no good reason.

My clearest recollection about the first day John and I spent together was that we laughed a lot. John loved to tell jokes and I loved to laugh at them. One went like this:

> Max's friends decided to hire a stripper for his ninetieth birthday. The stripper arrived at Max's door dressed only in a black bra, garter belt and black fishnet stockings. She announced, "I'm here for super sex." Max replied, "I'll take the soup!"

A great sense of humor had always been high up on my list for Mr. Right, but so were no other girlfriends and no life-threatening diseases. I guess that since I was no longer a spring chicken, a lot of my old requirements had gone out the window. I think it was similar for my elegantly turned-out mother when she was still single in her mid-thirties. In her salad days she would never have gone out with, much less married, a guy like my father, who cared so little about fashion that he wore white socks and who worked in a liquor store, even though he was a professional man, a pharmacist. I just had a feeling, as my mother did about my dad, that John was different and that I should give him some slack. Besides, I wasn't getting any younger either.

While we were walking around New York that first day, John clutched my hand in an odd way. "What is that?" I asked.

"My fraternity handshake."

"Which one?"

"ZBT."

"I was a little sister of ZBT."

My experience as a little sister of ZBT was a little like always a bridesmaid, never a bride. Instead of getting pinned to one of the brothers, the step just before engagement, I got my own little pin to show I was a fraternity mascot. I hung out with a lot of the guys. They liked me for my wit, my sarcasm, my soprano voice that on a good day sounded like Joan Baez's, my left-leaning politics, a priority in those days, but I was chubby and couldn't make my hair poker straight so they weren't interested in me romantically. I sang folk songs with them and watched *The Wizard of Oz* with them, but rarely danced with them or dated them. Now I finally got my chance to date a ZBT, only getting pinned at this late date was probably out of the question.

The Simon and Garfunkel concert was next, the ostensible reason for our meeting. I first saw Simon and Garfunkel in my sophomore year in college. I was on the entertainment committee for homecoming. It was just on the cusp of the real sixties for me, which were filled with teach-ins and protests. It was the calm before the anti-Vietnam storm. And I was, as I had been in high school, Miss Goody Two Shoes Student Government Girl. I was going out on a limb proposing Simon and Garfunkel for the homecoming concert. They were just one-hit wonders then— everyone my age knew "The Sounds of Silence." I had both of their albums. I played the vinyls until I had each of their songs memorized. So, Simon and Garfunkel came to homecoming along with Dick Gregory, whose most popular riff at the time was about Lyndon Johnson's getting barbecue sauce on the abdominal scar he exhibited to the world following gall bladder surgery. After Gregory performed, Paul Simon and Art Garfunkel mingled with us at intermission. They were regular kids like us, just a little older. My crush on Simon was deflated when I noticed that he was a head shorter than I. The coup at the homecoming concert, which took place at the Syria Mosque, Pittsburgh's mosaic answer to Carnegie Hall, was Simon and Garfunkel's introduction of their not-yet-released album, "Parsley, Sage, Rosemary and Thyme," which featured songs like "Feeling Groovy," "For Emily Whenever I May Find Her" and the title track. We were among the first to hear those songs.

Simon and Garfunkel songs reminded me of a string of boyfriends I had fallen in and out of love with. Was John just another link in that much too long chain?

The Halloween 1993 concert that John and I attended was held not in the cavernous Madison Square Garden but in the new gray-carpeted Paramount Theater in the depths of the Garden complex. Our seats were fifteenth row center. The concert was superb. The first half was devoted to songs made popular by Simon and Garfunkel, the second celebrated Simon's incredible oeuvre influenced by Brazilian and African music. Much had changed since homecoming with Simon and Garfunkel and with me. Garfunkel's voice, although still sweet, was not the perfect instrument it had been twenty-five years before. Simon, though, had written more varied, richer songs with more nuanced lyrics. The concert was a standout, the kind that because of wonderful deliveries and a large dose of nostalgia, sends you out singing.

When we left the Garden, I told John that I had a premonition that we would see someone with a beanie topped with a tiny propeller. I'm sure John had one of those "Who is this person and why am I with her?" moments. When we got on the number 9 subway to the Upper West Side, there he was, a guy with a propeller on his beanie, a guy with a hat. Now maybe you could say it wasn't much of a premonition. This was New York after all and it was Halloween. But there he was, just as I envisioned him. We laughed about my Halloween prescience. All seemed magical, but John was leaving for Toronto the next day.

We kissed as John got into the taxi. I didn't know if I would see him again.

Arizona

John and I talked daily after our New York trip even though base-ball season was over. Soon we were planning a trip for John's win-ter break. The Girl with the Hat apparently had other hats to buy or other fish to fry and didn't want to go away for Christmas, at least she told John she didn't want to go away with him.

December arrived before I knew it and I met John at the Phoenix Airport. He warned me before the trip that Christmas was very difficult for him and he would likely be out of sorts for much of the vacation because his dad had died on Christmas day several years before. The female Woody Allen had met a male ver-sion of herself and we were going to try to navigate the already impossible landscape of late-in-life love together.

I made most of the travel arrangements. John, though, picked one of the hotels, a New Age spa in Sedona that was our first stop. Now all of us Baby Boomers have soft spots in our hearts for any old thing that smacks of the sixties, so I was looking forward to reliving the part of my life that I and other members of my generation consider to be, with apologies to William Wyler, the best years of our lives. The spa was housed in a geodesic dome à la Buckminster Fuller, a huge cement ball. We had what was clearly the best room in the place, next to an indoor waterfall and garden. The waterfall clattered through the night and had the unmistakable and not at all New Age smell of chlorine. The waterfall posed an added problem for me. "What's wrong?" John asked when I got out of bed for the third time at about three in the morning.

"I have to pee again."

"You just went. Do you feel okay?"

"I'm fine. I just have to go."

"You're sure you're okay?" Wasn't this the concerned response I always wanted from a man?

"I'm fine, really. It's just the waterfall. My mother started to toilet train me at fourteen months, way before it was popular to start early. The way she did it was to turn on the faucet. So now running water, even rain, makes me want to go."

"Maybe we should change rooms?"

"I don't think so. I think you got the nicest one here. I'll be fine," I said as I started on my trek to the bathroom at the end of the hallway. My nostalgia for the sixties was turning into a yearning for nineties comfort.

One night we had dinner at the spa in a communal room on the second floor. Every hippie from Sedona and the surrounding area converged there. Now I really felt trapped in the sixties, which now seemed to be better in the abstract than in reality. Although I remembered the decade as a wonderful part of my life, somehow being stuck there thirty years later wasn't quite as appealing.

The perfect example of someone who wasn't stuck in one decade or another but who moved almost too patly from one to another was John's first cousin, Jerry Rubin. Yes, that Jerry Rubin. John and Jerry had grown up together in Cincinnati. They were born only a few weeks apart. Jerry went off to head the Youth International Party (the Yippies) with Abbie Hoffman in Berkeley. John went to graduate school at Harvard, married his first love when he was in his early twenties and divorced her after about a year. The Yippies organized rallies against the Vietnam War, the most notorious one at the Democratic National Convention in Chicago in 1968. Jerry, Abbie and six others were charged as the Chicago 8. They soon were on trial as the Chicago 7 since the only African American among them, Bobby Seale, was banned from the courtroom.

In the seventies Rubin hit on the idea of networking and arranged huge parties at Studio 54 in Manhattan where erstwhile hippies could bring their business cards and make contacts. Meanwhile John had moved to Canada with his second wife, Judy, had a baby, Jesse, and started his career as a film professor. In the 1980s Jerry became involved with investments and the stock market. John divorced his second wife, headed the film department at York University and met The Girl with the Hat. At the beginning of the 1990s Rubin was an entrepreneur, the head of a company selling health food. He never made it to the New Millennium. In his mid-fifties he was hit by a car crossing Wiltshire Boulevard in L.A., his decades-younger girlfriend, Tiffany, at his side. Bobby Seale did make it to the new century, selling barbecue sauce in my hometown.

Sedona, or the knowledge that John had The Girl with the Hat at home, I'm not sure which, made me very emotional. That perhaps is an understatement. It would be more accurate to say that I cried most of the time we were there. This was particularly odd since usually I was no crybaby. On our first morning in Sedona I was happy to escape the New Age spa. We went out to have breakfast in a diner. It wasn't really a diner. It was a storefront in a strip mall with the word "DINER" emblazoned on the plate glass window. We grabbed a table. I sat down and started to cry. "What's wrong?" John asked.

"I don't know. Maybe it's just because I didn't get much sleep last night," I answered.

They happened again and again, my crying jags. The last time was on our last day in Sedona on the Pink Jeep Tour, a perilous journey up and down mountains. Again, for no obvious reason, I began to cry. "What now?" John was progressively less sympathetic with each emotional outburst."

"I'm not sure."

Later in the tour the driver, when he wasn't carefully careening over the cliffs, told us that the Native Americans who originally settled in this part of Arizona thought there were vortexes, strong magnetic fields, that exerted a God-like pull and they prayed there. Some people think, he told us, that the vortexes bring out strong feelings even today in people who are visiting. John and I looked at each other. I wasn't sure either of us bought it. While all of this business about the vortexes and their effect on emotions might be true, it would be hard to discount my distress over The Girl with the Hat and my unenviable second-rate position in John's affections. Being in second place would be enough to make any unmarried only child cry.

Just before we left Sedona, to add to the otherworldly feel of our vacation, John got a call from a woman he had met at an Esalen autobiography workshop run by Spalding Gray. She was calling to give him a gift of an astrological reading by someone named Linda in Tempe. Two years before the workshop she attended with John, the woman and her fiancé had attended another Esalen workshop, "Letting Go and Having Fun." After that workshop her intended went to his weekend house somewhere on the East Coast, went out on a boat, tied the anchor to his foot and jumped overboard. In retrospect, all of this was made even more eerie by the mysterious disappearance and apparent suicide of Spalding Gray himself in 2004, likely a jump into the deep off of the Staten Island Ferry.

We made our way to Tempe, a detour on our way to Tucson. We stopped to see Linda in her suburban tract house, not the place you would expect to find an astrologer. The house was a wall-to-wall carpeted split-level surrounded by golf courses populated by senior citizens in brightly colored clothes, playing assiduously, as if their lives depended on it.

Linda saw us separately. I figured as long as I was there I would get a reading too. I have always had a superstitious streak and astrology appealed to me. John went first and I wandered around the tract homes wondering who the astrologer talked with between readings. What would she say to John? Would she tell him that he should be in love with the woman who had paid for the reading? Or with The Girl with the Hat? I doubted that she would have told him to wind up with me, or if she had, that he would have listened, because at that point both of us likely thought that Arizona had been a mistake.

When it was my turn Linda told me, "There is a foreigner in your future." Was Canada a foreign country to her? Philadelphia was foreign to this suburban enclave. Almost every woman that I have spoken with since who was in her forties when she consulted an astrologer was told that she would marry a foreigner. Must be that the astrologers figure that the term is open to interpretation and if by forty you haven't found someone in your own backyard, maybe there's someone somewhere else in the universe for you.

Neither of us divulged much about our readings except apparently Linda told John that he would marry a foreigner too. Either the stars were aligned so that each of us would marry a foreigner but not necessarily each other, or Linda figured that since we were on vacation together and were technically foreigners to each other—although not really, since John was originally from Cincinnati—that it was a pretty safe prediction.

Tucson was next on our itinerary. The first place we stayed was in the middle of the desert, but a desert that was fast turning into a suburb. We stayed in a bed and breakfast with a hot tub and artist hosts. I had stopped crying. There were challenging hiking trails nearby. I noticed that John couldn't hike as long as I, and that he became winded easily. I didn't think much of it. I attributed it to the nine-year difference in our ages. I didn't think it had anything to do with his kidneys wearing out. Soon after we arrived at the B&B, John sank into a funk. Christmas day, the anniversary of his father's death, was the next day. While browsing in the hostelry's tiny library, I noticed a memoir, one that I had never heard of, *The Invention of Solitude,* even though it was by my favorite author, Paul Auster. An earlier guest had apparently abandoned the book. I loved Auster's novels, which invariably explored the role of chance in his characters' lives. The book I found in Tucson was about Auster's father's dying, and I had found it just at the time John was struggling with his dad's death.

Our next stop was The Arizona Inn, near the center of Tucson. There were no vortexes there, but John and I fought constantly over why he wouldn't give up The Girl with the Hat. I had by then completely given up any blasé attitude about my competition.

I had always wanted to have a fireplace in my house. Oh, my psychiatrist had a field day with that one. Whenever I went on vacation I opted for a hotel room with a fireplace. I booked a room with a fireplace at the Arizona Inn. My fascination with fires was all the more incomprehensible considering the way I lost my virginity.

On my twenty-second birthday I realized that I was the last of my friends who was a virgin and resolved to find someone as soon as I could and get my deflowering over with. I happened to go to Cambridge a few weeks later and there on a soapbox at an anti-war rally in Harvard Square was an old flame. He was exhorting the crowd to urge Richard Nixon to get the hell out of Vietnam. I decided that he would be "it" and invited him to Philadelphia for the next weekend. I took him on a tour of the University of Pennsylvania, where I was on the verge of getting a terminal master's degree in English, a kind of terminal cancer for academics. He felt at home because right under the nose of founder Ben Franklin's statue another anti-war rally was under way. He paid more attention to the rally than to me. I didn't care. I was on a mission.

After the demonstration ended I asked him to meet me in an hour at my apartment on Rittenhouse Square. The building I lived in, a beige brick high rise, had, along with many of its dowager occupants, fallen on hard times. I tried to make the encounter as romantic as my unsophisticated twenty-two year old mind could imagine, so I bought wine, cheese and candles. I hadn't had much to drink since my junior year of college when, to keep up with my date, I drank half a fifth of Four Roses with a bathtub beer chaser, and passed out.

I thought the wine might put him in the mood. He hadn't seemed to be in the mood earlier that day. He had barely talked to me. When he did, mainly he talked about himself. Nevertheless, I was undaunted as I placed candles strategically around my living room and lit them. I shared the large L-shaped apartment with a disaffected social work student. It was only 10:00 p.m., but she was already asleep in the bedroom.

The doorbell rang. This was it. I opened the door, kissed him on the cheek and ushered him in. "Would you like some wine?"

"I'd rather have some dope."

"I don't have any."

"Too bad."

"Let's sit over there." I probably didn't have to say that, since there was only one place to sit in the bare living room, a single bed with foam bolsters that my roommate and I used as a makeshift couch. It was the same bed I had slept on as a child.

We didn't talk much. We both knew why we were there. In a very perfunctory way we "did it," in the true slam-bam-thank-you-ma'am meaning of "did it," as unmemorable as that, devoid of foreplay. For me it was over in a flash after a stab of pain. He immediately went to the bathroom to wash off.

I lay there wondering if that was all there was to it. And then I smelled a strange odor. Was it the smell that went along with the loss of a maidenhead? It smelled like burning rubber. It was burning rubber. A candle had tipped over and was scorching one of the twin bolsters on my childhood bed. Not just a singe, mind you. Soon there were flames, red and yellow tongues dancing and lashing the pillow. The fire mesmerized me. I admired its beauty. Actually, I was in shock. I had just roughly lost my virginity, and my apartment was on fire. When I came to my senses, I ran over to the sink, filled a teakettle with water and doused the flames. The fire went out, leaving only suffocating smoke and a putrid smell.

Suddenly there was incessant pounding on the door. I dressed quickly. My roommate, who was awakened either by the smell or the pounding, stumbled bleary-eyed out of the bedroom in her pink flannel pajamas. My erstwhile Prince Charming ran out of the bathroom and threw on his pants. I opened the door and there they were—five firemen, huge guys as big as Eagles defensive linemen. They were decked out head to toe in black rubber gear. The one in the front, the biggest of them all, was brandishing a huge ax, like the ones in bad horror movies. "Is there a fire here, lady?" one of them asked. I pointed to my childhood bed and the soaked, smelly bolster. All five went to investigate.

"It was an accident," I explained.

"Be more careful next time," the one with the ax said.

"Believe me, I will be."

Almost as soon as we arrived in the room at The Arizona Inn I asked John, "Can we make a fire?"

"I have a fireplace at home and they make a big mess."

"I love fires."

"Then make one yourself."

"I'm not really sure how to do it."

I tried to followed the directions the hotel provided, but I forgot to open the flue. Because I hadn't had much experience with indoor fires, unless you count the time with the bolster, and no experience with flues, the room filled with smoke. John, who was already peeved about my crying jags and my cross-examination about why he hung on to The Girl with the Hat, was furious. "I knew this would happen."

"So why didn't you make the fire."

"Because I didn't want one."

We managed to put the fire out with a few buckets of water. All of our clothes smelled like smoke. We decided to go to the movies to give our room time to air out.

I was acting as the navigator and got us horribly lost. This was unusual because since childhood I had been a human compass and rarely lost my way—on the roads, that is. I realized that I was still furious with John because of The Girl with the Hat. We arrived fifteen minutes late at the multiplex but saw the movie we had planned to anyway. At the end of the credits was an acknowledgment of Paul Auster, the novelist of chance.

After the movie we decided to explore downtown Tucson. We stopped in a jewelry store. Since no one else offered, I decided to buy myself a necklace with a turquoise heart suspended from multiple silver strands. "Are there any more like that?" John asked the saleswoman, for The Girl with the Hat, I presumed.

"I'll look," the saleswoman volunteered. She went into a room at the rear of the store and came back empty-handed. Because there was a God or an astrologer, there were no more.

"Can I see those?" He was pointing to unwieldy mosaic earrings in putrid shades of brown, green and orange. The woman behind the counter brought them out of the case and placed them on a swatch of blue velvet. "What do you think of them?" John asked, looking in my direction.

"They're beautiful," I lied.

When we left the store I let John have it. No more forlorn crying about being second best. "How could you?"

"How could I what?"

"Buy a present for someone else when I was right there?"

"I never hid the fact that I have a girlfriend."

He had a point.

By the time we got to the penultimate stop, on the west side of Tucson, John and I were barely civil to each other. This was by far the strangest of the Tucson hostelries. A couple ran the place. He was a Yale graduate and did something with investments, and they had grown children who had moved out. So they had decided to open a bed and breakfast in their house. Bed was the operative word. There was only one guest suite. There was only one bed. It was like staying with your extended family, only it was a family you didn't know. We had breakfast with them at their dining room table. All of this was made more difficult because John and I were hardly speaking and we had to put on a good front for our new family.

Next came Phoenix, the end of our vacation and, I thought, the end of our relationship. We were staying at a fleabag motel near the airport, my worst gaffe of the trip. John went to visit relatives in Phoenix. He left me in the fleabag, likely because the relatives knew that he and The Girl with the Hat were an item, and he would be hard pressed to explain me.

We said goodbye at the airport. I thought, "Good riddance."

ULTIMATUM

John and I talked some in January. It wasn't the same easy banter. Against the better judgment of a few of my male friends, I told John I didn't want to see him until he got rid of The Girl with the Hat. Then he uttered my most-hated pop psychology phrase, "I hear you." I hung up.

Valentine's Day. One of the most dreaded days on the single woman's calendar, second only to New Year's Eve. Valentine's Day had been a trying day for me ever since I was eleven. That year I decided to have a Valentine's Day party and told each of my friends to ask a boy. I invited a very special boy for myself. I went on a shopping trip with my mother to buy a dress for the party. My mother threatened to take me to the chubby department to buy an outfit. I begged her not to. Instead we went to a store that specialized in pre-teen clothes. I picked out a white party dress with silver thread running through it and a big red bow at the collar that never seemed to stay tied. The dress was very Valentine's Day appropriate, even if it was a little tight across my midriff.

The time came for the party. The basement was all decked out in red and white crepe paper. There were paper plates full of potato chips and pretzels. There was also the requisite plate of candy Valentine hearts that said, "Be Mine" and "I Luv U." My girlfriends arrived one by one, with their boyfriends. My red bow came undone. My date never arrived. My father, who rarely showed any anger, was furious. "What is that boy's name and where does he live?" I couldn't answer. I helped my mother clean up, went upstairs and cried myself to sleep.

When I was a sophomore at the Philadelphia High School for Girls, Miss Fugate (the same woman I credit for my language skills at the Montreal Film Festival) invited twenty girls in my class to a Valentine's Day social, an afternoon get-together with boys. It was odd that Miss Fugate should be organizing such an outing, since she was a stern, never-married woman in her fifties. She was an incredible teacher but no-nonsense. Unapproachable. I was the only one of my friends who hadn't been invited, a situation I had become achingly used to since seventh grade. I still hadn't shed my baby fat, and in a desperate attempt to tame my curly mane decades before Carrie Bradshaw on *Sex and the City* made wild curls popular, I had had my hair cut short in what could only be described as a lamb cut. I guess that Miss Fugate, who was trying to pick the cream of the crop, didn't think that I rose to the top of the group or even to the middle.

For some reason the shy part of myself when it came to postpubescent boys didn't carry over to any other part of my life. In most other areas I was downright assertive. Somehow these two parts of my personality were coming together over this social issue. I gathered the gumption to confront my teacher. Now Miss

Fugate was forbidding, so my confrontation was no mean feat. She was about five foot three, compact, and stood perfectly straight. I was probably slouching when I summoned up the courage to talk to her because I was five foot six at the time and she seemed much taller than I. She had gray-blond hair even shorter than my lamb cut and wore her glasses suspended around her neck. She had eagle eyes that always appeared to be darting here and there. She didn't miss anything. My only real asset in my conversation with my French teacher was that she liked me because I had a real knack for the language. I walked up to her after class. She peered at me through her glasses, which were then perched near the tip of her nose. "All of my friends are going. Why not me?" She immediately knew what I meant.

"There was a limit to how many girls could go...," and taking pity on my stricken look, she seemed to change her mind in mid-sentence, "...oh, I'm sure it won't matter. I'll add your name to the list."

I was elated and panicked at the same time. I had given myself another chance to succeed on the social scene after many failed attempts in junior high. The dance was at Girard College for Boys. In 1848 Stephen Girard, a prominent Philadelphia shipbuilder, left money in his will to start a school for white orphan boys. Years after my experience there and decades after segregated schools should have been allowed to exist, private or not, Girard's will was broken and the "white" was removed. Even later orphan girls were admitted.

I had done it. I had persuaded Miss Fugate to let me have at those orphan boys. My mother was less than overjoyed. I don't think she saw my future with an orphan who lived in a residential school. She was probably not happy about my going to what she thought was an unsafe neighborhood to meet my orphan. And I'm sure she knew that if I did meet my orphan he probably wouldn't be Jewish, and her grandchildren, the products of me and the orphan, wouldn't have a *Bris* or a *Bar* or *Bat Mitzvah*.

Maybe my mother's lack of enthusiasm for the Girard College social explains the outfit we wound up buying. There wasn't much time for me to find just the right thing, less than twenty-four hours. I refused to wear anything I already owned. This would be a new beginning for my social life. I needed a new outfit.

At my insistence we went to The Marianne Shoppe, a store that hawked trendy, cheap clothes. Lots of the stores in those days appended that extra "pe" to shop to give the lower end a pseudo Old English feel. My mother and I had never been to a store like The Marianne Shoppe before. She prided herself in buying me high-end clothes wholesale. Marianne was decidedly low-end at retail. Maybe my mother thought that if I was going to meet orphans I should dress like one.

My weight in those days fluctuated between 110 and 150. I would go to camp in the summer, shed forty pounds and spend the next few months packing the weight right back on by gorging on M&M's and Goldenberg's Peanut Chews in my parents' store. It was the beginning of February when we shopped for the Girard social outfit. I was almost at my fattest. I settled on a black wide-pleated cotton skirt that accentuated my full hips. Black was a good idea—the wide pleats weren't. By far my worst fashion faux pas at The Marianne Shoppe, and maybe the worst one ever committed there, was what I chose next. I picked out a red-and-white-checked short-sleeved shirt with ruffles around the neck, sleeves and bottom. The bottom ruffle hit me in the widest part of my hips. When I tried on the outfit I thought it was great. My mother said, "It makes you look fat." The more I looked at the outfit after I got home the less sure I was about it.

The Girard social was my stab at independence. I had made my own fate by wangling an invitation. Now I had chosen my own outfit in spite of how fat my mother thought it made me look. She always told me how fat I looked, and at this time of year she was certainly right. I was fat and I looked fat, and by the time camp rolled around in a few months I would look even fatter.

The big day came. It was the middle of February in 1962 and there I was in what actually looked like a spring clown costume, complete with the ruffle around the neck. All of my friends were in their Villager outfits, then de rigueur for winter in high school—raspberry, lime and blueberry sherbet-colored wool skirts with matching sweaters. And I was decked out in my spring clown finery. I didn't fully realize my fashion victim-hood until I glanced around at my friends waiting to get on the bus that would take us to Girard College in their color-coordinated wool outfits and their straight shiny hair. And there I was in my sheep cut. A lamb in clown's clothing. There was nothing I could do but have a stiff upper lip and get on the bus. Surely there would be a fashion-unconscious plump orphan for me.

We arrived at Girard and piled into a huge room at the College. It was called a College for some unknown reason, another of Stephen Girard's quirks besides sex and race discrimination, even though it was really a high school. The room we landed in was dark-wood-paneled with a row of suspended lights, like the room in *Oliver Twist* where the foundlings got their gruel. This looked like the room where the Girard orphans got their gruel too. For the dance all of the dining tables and benches were moved against the wall, leaving a cavernous space in the center of the room. The darkness should have been an asset to me, but since I was the only one in primary colors I stood out. The orphans arrived. I moved as close to the wall as I could, banged into a gruel bench and sat down. I sat there for two hours watching my friends mingle with the orphans. You would have thought there would have been something in orphan etiquette that would have

44

required the orphans to ask even a wallflower in clown attire to dance. No orphan even bothered to come to talk with me. I was so relieved when we were asked to get on the bus. My adventure with the orphans finally ended. I had failed again at yet another Valentine's party. I couldn't even make an orphan like me.

I was particularly vulnerable on Valentine's Day night 1994. I had spent the evening at a singles party. This was a special kind of singles party because not only did it feature the most desperate singles of both sexes—those who were willing to admit that they were dateless on Valentine's Day rather than staying home quietly like any other self-respecting single—but also because it was a precursor to the two-, four- and six-minute dates that became all the rage years later. After each course the single men would move to a different table to see if any of the single women were to their liking. After meeting an accountant who prided himself in never going to the movies, a doctor who hated lawyers and a man who claimed to be a private jet pilot but who really sold insurance, I was ready to go home and eat a gallon of Ben and Jerry's. (We Jewish girls don't usually drink all that much, but often drown our sorrows in something cold and creamy.)

Not two minutes after I walked through my door, the phone rang. John was calling. And was I tempted. A smart man with a sense of humor was on the phone. I hadn't met or spoken to anyone like that since I had given him my ultimatum. "Happy Valentine's Day," he said.

"Did you get rid of The Girl with the Hat?"

"No. I just called to see how you were and say Happy Valentine's Day."

"I'm not interested until you get rid of her."

I hung up. Where was The Girl with the Hat? Out on the town alone with her red hat? After I hung up, I couldn't believe what I had done, especially in the face of the mass of losers I had met at singles musical tables. What was I thinking? Isn't some attention from someone I'm compatible with better than nothing? No, I wanted it all. No more second best.

The Girl with the Hat was still ahead. I didn't want to play under those circumstances. I felt that I had lost a lot when I gave John my ultimatum, but my only-child self was unwilling to play second fiddle in an orchestra where The Girl with the Hat had the first chair. I grew up being, or at least I was supposed to be, the center of attention and might have been if my parents hadn't worked such long hours in the store and had ever been home. I had waited too long for Mr. Right. John was not my Mr. Right if he had a Ms. Wrong he wouldn't get rid of.

over the boardwalk

Then came the call from John in August, almost one year to the day after our street corner meeting. Before he could say anything, I asked, "Did you get rid of The Girl with the Hat?"

"I'm getting there but I'm not there yet. There was someone in between, she's a redhead, but I like you more."

"Great. So now there are The Girl with the Hat and The Little Redheaded Girl. Let me know when you get rid of both of them."

"Please, I really want to see you."

The Little Redheaded Girl was introduced to John by a Toronto friend who had met her on a vacation in some Central American country. John had been seeing her, while still involved with The Girl with the Hat, since sometime after that Valentine's Day phone call. John was bound and determined not to be left alone, as he had been so often by his parents, if the bottom fell out between him and The Girl with the Hat. He decided that he didn't want to see The Little Redheaded Girl anymore, or so he told me, because she had apparently exploded at her doorman for some insignificant slight. And so John was trying me again, convinced that I had better control over my anger, an apparent requisite for dealing with him. Now another obstacle was removed, even though I hadn't known it existed. I listened to all of this and again refused to see him.

Then John sent me a birthday card and in a weak moment (I had just turned forty-seven, which would cause weakness in any single unmarried woman), I relented, against my better judgment. I had the blessings of my male friends, who thought that at my age I couldn't afford to be so picky and that the ultimatum idea would never bring me happiness. Before I knew it John was coming to Philadelphia for the weekend. I was very excited about seeing him again but had a lot of trepidation. The Girl with the Hat hadn't been booted out of the picture. I wasn't sure if The Little Redheaded Girl was still a bleep on the radar.

It was late October, just about a year after our first date in New York. The first night John arrived, rather than discussing anything much, we went out with his friends Jay and Janis. I always wondered if they were checking me out to make sure that I was okay. Things went well at dinner. I thought I had passed the test. In fact Jay told John that I was the best thing that had happened to John in a long time.

The weather was unseasonably mild that weekend. We decided to drive to Atlantic City the next day and walk on the Boardwalk. John fell in love with the place. I had been in love with Atlantic City only briefly. In the 1940s and 1950s I had come with my parents to stay in my childless Aunt Gertie and Uncle Mike's rooming house with almost all of my extended family. For the first time I felt like I had brothers and sisters, even though I knew that they were only second cousins and that when the summer was over I would return to my house and they would return to theirs. By the time I was in my teens I felt I didn't belong in Atlantic City. Aunt Gertie was by then a widow and no longer had the rooming house. I had always been too shy to venture into the crowds of teenagers on the Boardwalk. That was for the more adventurous girls who were up to making out under the Boardwalk in Chelsea. I was much too self-conscious for the Boardwalk scene. Atlantic City became all the more unpleasant to me when the garish casinos replaced the beautiful early twentieth-century hotels that dotted the Boardwalk when I was a child.

Every time I walk by what was in my teen years that very social section of the Boardwalk, all those memories of not belonging flood back. I walked there with John that day in October.

I took him to the Atlantic City apartment my mother had left me in her will. It was a small studio in The Warwick, a 1940s era beige and brown eyesore that sat on the Boardwalk overlooking the ocean. The apartment itself was all powder blue—powder blue walls, powder blue carpet, powder blue sheets and towels. It was reminiscent of my monochromatic childhood bedroom. I felt sad whenever I went to the apartment. I felt as I did whenever I was around my mother—like something about me wasn't quite right—my hair, my clothes. My mother had already been dead for three years when I showed John the apartment, yet I still felt her presence there and continued to feel as if I were doing something wrong, especially that there was something wrong with the way I looked. My feeling in 1994 was an improvement over how I felt when my mother was alive. At least I only felt as if I looked unattractive or was doing something wrong when I was in the Atlantic City apartment. When my mother was alive I felt that way most of the time.

I had always been on the losing end of the competition with my mother. Aside from the band-boxy, never creased look she always had, there were all of those things she could do well and seemingly effortlessly. She was screamingly competent. She pretty much single-handedly ran the drugstore. My father filled the prescriptions. She did the rest—hiring the help and ordering everything in the store, from potato chips to the lipsticks my junior high nemeses shoplifted. She kept the books. She met with the accountant. In the limited time she had left, she was quite a good homemaker. The house was always spotless because she or someone she hired and vigilantly supervised kept it that way. She somehow found the time to shop for furniture and for clothes for everyone in the family. Except for The Marianne Shoppe she never shopped retail. "Any dummy," she always said, "can buy retail." Before there were discount malls, she turned up store after factory outlet that offered top quality goods at deep discount prices.

My mother had a great sense of color and style even into her seventies. She never left the house without every hair and seam in place. She was always beautifully dressed and color-coordinated. Her suit matched her gloves, shoes and purse.

And then there were the crafts. Rose could sew, knit and crochet. She could look at a sweater in a Ralph Lauren ad and duplicate it for me stitch for stitch, such good copies that had she done the copying recently, Lauren's knockoff police might have been after her.

Rose was no great shakes in the kitchen while I was growing up. She had neither time nor a decent role model for cooking. My maternal grandmother's specialty was chicken soup with an inch of fat congealed on top. After the store closed and her work duties lessened, my mother became a fine cook. She made matzo balls at Passover that swam delicately in her finely seasoned chicken soup. She learned how to bake and turned out delectable apple cakes.

In short, everything my mother touched was perfectly turned out—from her outfits to afghans to apple cakes. So you would think I would have inherited some of this prowess. Nope. I was as awkward with my hands as she was graceful. I always creased. If my clothes were mismatched I didn't much care. I must have inherited my father's white socks gene. Maybe a progeny like me had been my mother's worst nightmare when at first she refused to date my father because he wore white socks.

Figuring that she had successfully changed my father from a white-sock-wearing liquor store employee to a professional man who wore black socks, my mother never stopped trying to change me. The more she criticized my appearance, the more lackadaisical I became. I knew from a very early age that no matter what I did I couldn't compete with her gorgeous look and her competence in everything she touched. When I was around my mother she constantly reminded me where I was lacking. After years of these reminders, I knew I could never measure up and stopped trying. Academics were my ace in the hole. I was a success at school, schools of every kind, and put my energies there.

My mother's only wish for me was that I would get married, hopefully to someone Jewish, and give her grandchildren. Even during high school she would occasionally leave copies of the *Jewish Exponent* on my bed. This intensified when I was one of the few girls who returned from college without an engagement ring. The *Exponent,* like many other Jewish weeklies of the time, published engagement announcements titled "KAPLAN-GOLDBERG," with the picture of either Goldberg or Kaplan or both, a description of their college careers and, for the lucky few, their law school or medical school education, and the date they were to be married. "A September wedding is planned." These blurbs hurt me, yet my mother continued to place the *Exponent* on my bed opened to the "Engagements" section as if seeing Kaplan, a beautiful girl with poker-straight dark hair perfectly coiffed, the kind of girl who never wrinkles, would somehow motivate frizzy-haired, creasable me to go out, find a Dr. Goldberg, the son of Dr. and Mrs. Goldberg, and get married.

In my last year of college, in a kind of grown-up version of finding Tommy, my first grade boyfriend and the only gentile first grader in a flock of Jewish ones, I set my sights on the son of an Episcopal priest. He set his sights on me too, and we dated for a while. The first question my mother would ask when she called me at college was, "Are you dating?" My usual answer was "No." On the rare occasion that I said "Yes," she would follow up immediately with, "Is he Jewish?" The next question would inevitably be, "What does his father do?"

During my mainly dateless college years my mother Rose was as good as she had ever been at finding my most vulnerable spot and jabbing at the open dateless wound. I, who had been trained by the mistress of tearing open a wound, had become expert at, consciously or unconsciously, finding and exploiting my mother's most vulnerable spot. The preacher man's son was the opposite of the Jewish doctor son of a Jewish doctor my mother wanted for me, not just for me, but also to impress her friends who would read the engagement announcement in the *Exponent*. I told my mother about the very sweet son of a priest I was dating. She was speechless. I imagined the notice my parents would place in the Jewish weekly.

SALTZMAN-CHRISTIAN

Rose and Samuel Saltzman of Oxford Circle sadly announce the engagement of their ungrateful, rebellious daughter Joan Abby to Christopher Christian, son of the Reverend and Mrs. Nicolas

Christian of Pittsburgh. A fall wedding is planned at St. Stephen's Church, where Reverend Christian is an Episcopal priest.

The Saltzmans have omitted Joan's photograph because her hair was unruly on the day of the photo shoot and because she refused to wear makeup.

I decided sometime in the sixties, while being tortured with the *Jewish Exponent,* that if what my mother wanted me to do was to get married and have children, that would be the last thing I would do. That would show her. But she never gave up hope and always asked me who I was seeing and how it was going. I seldom told her. I rarely dated anyone Jewish. When I occasionally dated a Jewish guy I was surprised at how much I had in common with him. I just wasn't going to give my mother the satisfaction of getting what she wanted and so I didn't give myself the satisfaction either.

And so Dr. and Mrs. Goldberg continued their successful reign in the *Exponent* with their children's birth, *Bar Mitzvah* and engagement announcements, while my mother and I continued our forty-some-year spite contest.

My mother had been in perfect health except for a benign breast cyst and a stone-infested gall bladder until she was seventy-five years old. One day I got a call that she had been taken to the hospital from the same Atlantic City apartment I showed John. She had had a heart attack. There had been no warning. When I got to the hospital I found a much less formidable Rose. She looked so small and helpless in the bed. When she saw me she said, "How could this have happened to me?" She couldn't tolerate beta-blockers, the medication that would have prolonged her life. For the next five years my always independent, strong mother became progressively thinner and weaker. She was in and out of the hospital with increasingly worsening episodes of heart failure. She finally gave up her Oldsmobile, her last vestige of independence.

Shortly before Rose died I took her out for Mother's Day. I decided that it was important for us to have a heart-to-heart. I had a Michael Feinstein CD on in the car. She loved the Gershwin songs. We were on our way to Atlantic City so she could see the friends who had sustained her. I told her how she had made me feel growing up and that I knew that she didn't mean to, and that I understood it was difficult because she had so many responsibilities in the store. I told her I forgave her.

"I always thought I was such a good mother,." she replied.

Figuring that this was not the time to be amazed at a statement like that, I just said, "Never mind. I love you."

"I love you too."

In the last year of her life my mother just wouldn't let go. She didn't want to leave me "all alone in the world," as she described it. My dad had died years earlier. On a cold October day in 1991 I went to visit Rose in the hospital with my most recent non-Jewish boyfriend. "You don't have to hold on anymore, mom. I'll be fine. I love you."

"I love you so much."

"I know. Now you can let go." I kissed her on the forehead.

The next day she lapsed into a coma and died.

John had none of my associations with Atlantic City. He was from Cincinnati and Toronto, both landlocked places. The ocean was a wonder to him. He even liked the idea of the casinos. To me eyesores like the Taj Mahal and Caesar's were like the end of the world. I remembered John Houseman of the American Repertory Theater, who was a Bar Association speaker at the annual convention of the Philadelphia bench and bar in Atlantic City, chosen for his role in *The Paper Chase,* a movie about law school (and not because of his theatrical work or his association with Orson Welles and his famed radio program *War of the Worlds,* where they cried wolf about the arrival of Martians in New Jersey and caused a furor). At the convention, Houseman remarked that when he saw the tourists pouring out of the Atlantic City bus station, it struck him that this was what it must look like in hell—he said Hades—when everyone pours in.

John and my last stop in Atlantic City that October day was at The White House, not a new casino that looked like the president's residence in Washington, D.C., but a legendary hoagie joint thought by some to be the best on the East Coast. Impossibly huge amounts of capicolla, mozzarella cheese and salami were stuffed on to homemade rolls, slathered with oil and mayonnaise and topped with chunks of onions and peppers. John went off his low-protein diet that day. I think that The White House was where I won what was then available of John's heart.

When we said goodbye, Ms. Ultimatum—as I was by then probably known to John and his friends—had yet another one. "Next time we get together, I want it to be in Toronto." Of course, this created a difficult problem for John since The Girl with the Hat, albeit with her hat somewhat askew, was still in the picture. What would she say or do? Would I be in danger? Would it be like in *Goldfinger* where James Bond's nemesis lets his hat go and decapitates his target?

THE GIRL WITH THE HAT
COMES OUT OF THE CLOSET

Still firmly in my way was The Girl with the Hat when out of the blue I got a call from John, a week after he left Philadelphia. Seems The Girl with the Hat had found another girl with a hat, her Yiddish teacher and, *oy,* they had fallen in love in some *meshugah* hat-over-heels kind of way and were riding off into the sunset together. John said that he and the first girl with the hat had gone to a Chinese restaurant near his house where she broke the news. They both cried and vowed that they would continue to be best friends.

That The Girl with the Hat had a girlfriend came as a shock to John until he thought about it for a while and talked to his friends. None of them were surprised. And after he thought about it for a while longer, neither was he. The fact that it was all clear to him in hindsight didn't stop him from being profoundly hurt.

But for me this very late-twentieth-century kind of event was the beginning of a relationship that, for the first time in my life, had the prospect of becoming a real one. And I had to face whether I really wanted a relationship as well as whether I wanted to hook my star to a very sick man. By this time John's energy was dissipating. He would tire after walking a few blocks. He fell asleep early in the evening. He would push himself to stay awake but when he did, he was irritable.

For me, John's illness would have been a good excuse to run away, but for some reason I didn't. I couldn't figure out where I had gone wrong. I had done my usual. Pick Mr. Wrong, someone unobtainable, loaded with baggage. But wait. Now he was turning into something else, not exactly a Disney Prince Charming, but the baggage was falling away, valise by valise.

I went to Toronto at the end of November. John was not completely comfortable with my visiting. He was worried we would run into The Girl with the Hat or her friends or relatives and it would be awkward.

I had heard wonderful things about Toronto. When I cleared customs, there was John standing behind a transparent partition, smiling and clinking his keys against the glass to get my attention. Then we got into the car and I saw a spanking new skyline, awfully tall and way too modern for me, a girl who came from a city full of eighteenth-century houses where, until a few years before, no building could be higher than William Penn's statue perched atop a nineteenth-century City Hall—the same statue that only a year before had worn the Phillies cap of shame. Toronto had grown up with the migration of banks and businesses from Montreal in the twentieth century, because English-speaking Canadians feared Quebec would secede and worried that a French Canadian takeover would destroy business life as they had known it.

Toronto seemed much too clean to me and not at all intense. For all of the problems with big Eastern American cities, they each have a strong heartbeat that keeps the adrenaline flowing. Toronto was bland. It seemed to have no soul. The city John lived in was veiled in gray. In the winter, which lasted from October until May, the sun rarely shone. It got darker earlier than I was used to. Even in November the temperature was bone-chilling.

Like the climate, people on the street were chilly. They seemed uncomfortable talking with strangers. In Philadelphia, Washington and New York, in spite of stereotypes to the contrary, people smile and are helpful. Not so in Toronto. John's friends, though, were welcoming. His closest friend, Harvey, arrived with a bouquet of flowers when he came to meet us at the Studio Café at The Four Seasons.

By the time I left Toronto, after hiding and going out after dark to avoid The Girl with the Hat, John and I were planning a trip to California.

TWO BUNCH PALMS AND THE BUS TO LAX

Like true film aficionados we picked a vacation destination that was a location for a vacation in *The Player,* a Robert Altman movie—Two Bunch Palms in Desert Hot Springs, California.

We started out in San Francisco. John loved the city, had visited many times and even spent a sabbatical or two there. I was just happy to see City Lights Bookstore again, a haunt of Lawrence Ferlinghetti and Allen Ginsberg. I had had a love affair with Ferlinghetti's poem, "A Coney Island of the Mind," in high school and had read most of Ginsberg's poetry.

We drove down the coast to Santa Cruz, Carmel, Pebble Beach. We skipped San Simeon, as we did with many places, because John had been there with The Girl with the Hat and was still too raw from the breakup to revisit. I had wanted to visit Hearst's mansion to see if Orson Welles got it right in *Citizen Kane.*

By Santa Barbara we were not getting along. I was tired of being told we couldn't visit some place or another I had never seen because of nostalgia over The Girl with the Hat. I was also tired of John's being inconsolably morose when we did go to a place that he had gone with The Girl, who had likely been sporting some hat or another at the time. We stopped at The Four Seasons in Santa Barbara for brunch. John disappeared from the table for an hour and returned with no explanation. I was suspicious that he had been talking to his new best friend and I was furious. She had been present like a specter throughout our vacation, a ghost with a hat. John was defensive and angry with me for being suspicious, and I became more suspicious.

Then we drove to Two Bunch Palms. Soon after we arrived we had a major blowup. I told him if he didn't start paying attention to me—he had stopped doing that soon after I confronted him in Santa Barbara—that I was going to go home. This kind of confrontation was not my usual way of dealing with the guys I dated. Once I decided that I liked them, I was usually so grateful that they were hanging around no matter how badly they treated me that I suffered in silence. Not this time. I didn't know then that John's biggest fear was being abandoned, although I should have since I knew that John had been left at home, first by his father and then by both of his parents. His reluctance to end things with The Girl with the Hat until he had another girl firmly in hand should also have been another clue to his Achilles' heel. My threat to leave had hit a nerve. Suddenly John's attitude changed.

He became warm and caring. He recited love poems and sang songs to me. He held my hand. He admitted that he knew I was special on our first date when I sang him all of the words of one of his favorite union songs, "Joe Hill." He loved that I knew a lot about movies. The Two Bunch Palms ambience didn't hurt. Low-slung buildings and small villas dotted the lush green lawn. I always thought of the place as a kind of old-time sanitarium like the ones you would see in the 1940s movies where Bette Davis or Claudette Colbert would go to recover from tuberculosis or a nervous breakdown. In the midst of the lawn was a huge pond stocked with gold, black and white koi. We spent most of our day there camped on reclining chairs, dozing and watching the fish. There were hot springs on the property that fed two large pools of varying hot temperatures. After lollydazing on the chairs and watching the fish we would slowly make our way to the hot springs and soak in the pools until we couldn't take the heat anymore. A long afternoon nap followed. Once we made the mistake of leaving the spa property to go to Palm Springs to find some nightlife. The spell was broken. When we returned to Two Bunch Palms after an evening away, we vowed never to leave the spa until we were forced to.

We had been promised as part of the hotel rate a continental breakfast. We sat on a sun-filled terrace laced with bougainvilleas. We expected the usual for breakfast—coffee, orange juice, and if we were lucky, croissants. Not Two Bunch Palms. We had our choice of fresh raspberry, coconut or grapefruit juice. There was fresh fruit in abundance, croissants, brioches, exotic pastries and granola. Thanks to Robert Altman and his movie, and thanks to an abandonment scare, we had truly found paradise.

Our last stop was in Malibu in a slightly rundown motel but with a wonderful view of the Pacific Ocean. We celebrated New Year's Eve at 9:00 p.m., since it was midnight on the East Coast, ate avocado sandwiches, drank Martinelli's Sparkling Cider and went to bed early.

We left for LAX, L.A.'s airport, on New Year's Day, dropped off the car and picked up the National shuttle to the terminals. As we were on our way to our respective planes, sitting as close as we could, our hands entwined, John leaned over to me and said,

"I love you." Since less than a week before I was ready to throw him and the bathwater out, I was taken aback and didn't answer. Also, men don't say "I love you" to single women over forty-five every day. I just wasn't used to hearing those three little words I had been promised by all of the romantic movies I had ever seen. John repeated, "I love you." Now I identified another emotion besides surprise. I wasn't sure what it was at the time. In hindsight I think that the emotion was fear. I must have decided it was about time to ignore the fear and get on with my life. I don't think any of this was conscious. There were only a few seconds between John's second "I love you" and my reply.

"I love you too," I answered and kissed him.

Just then we pulled up to the US Airways terminal and, as with all long-distance romances, we had to get on separate planes and part.

THE EX-WIFE AND THE SON

John and I bounced back and forth between Philadelphia and Toronto from January until May. Because of John's teaching schedule he could leave Toronto in May and not return until September.

I knew I had my work cut out for me before John came for an extended stay. First I had to do something with the Atlantic City apartment to transform it from baby blue to neutral. Walls were painted white. Brown carpets replaced the baby blue ones. Wicker furniture made it look more livable.

Then there was the psychological part. John was not used to a big American city. All of those years of living in Canada made him the opposite of streetwise—his wallet often stuck out of his back pocket, ripe for the picking. He didn't know who to avoid when he walked down the street. He had none of the defensive skills that someone used to the dangers of a big American city knew intuitively. He complained that Philadelphia was dangerous; that all the local news showed was one heinous crime after another. Because I had lived most of my life in Philadelphia, I took the dangers and dodging them as facts of life.

John complained a lot about Philadelphia and for the first few months he lived in Philly in the summer of 1995, he lauded Toronto. Toronto was cleaner. Toronto was practically crime free. On several occasions I became so tired of his badmouthing my hometown I urged him to go back to that idyllic city up north. He didn't. Truth was, although he wasn't thrilled with Philadelphia, he loved Atlantic City. He wanted to go to the cozy little studio by the beach whenever he could. I was less thrilled with Atlantic City because I had to battle my mother's ghost each time we went there. We burned sage, which is supposed to purge bad spirits. That didn't work. Whenever I went to that apartment my mother's spirit was there, letting me know that she could still see all of my flaws.

After a few months of scurrying between Philadelphia and Atlantic City, the graduation of John's son, Jesse, was next on our agenda. Jesse was graduating from Concordia University in Montreal. I was eager to get back to the city where John and I had met, but I didn't see this trip, which involved meeting his son and his ex-wife Judy, as a carefree romantic holiday.

I had not yet met John's only child. I worried whether Judy and Jesse would like me or even tolerate me. I had heard a raft of stories about wicked stepchildren, and I worried that I would get one.

John and Judy separated when Jesse was about fourteen. Judy was nice enough to me but I realized that the split was less than amicable when she said, "John always finds such nice women. I can't figure it out."

Jesse, who was at the time about five foot eight, thin with hair down to the middle of his back, reminded me of a kind of latter-day hippie. He had even taken a year off to follow the Grateful Dead. Since I had been a hippie myself, that was just all right with me. Jesse was bright and thoughtful. We had a lot in common. His major was comparative religion. Mine had been philosophy. We were both only children.

So, in the end Jesse and I got along famously. With my concerns gone about whether Jesse would accept me, I was free to obsess about what else might adversely affect my relationship with John. We were getting along. There were no insurmountable problems. His health was an issue, but I thought we could deal with that even if some day he had to go on dialysis. I had a real relationship at last. I was just waiting for the other shoe to drop.

Yahrtzeit in cooperstown

On our way home from Jesse's graduation, we decided to spend a few days in Lake George. When we got near Lake George, first we saw one motorcycle, then five, then hundreds. There was a motorcycle conclave. Everywhere there were thousands of huge cycles barreling toward us or humming behind. John was driving and I wouldn't let him stop anywhere. There were "No Vacancy" signs on all of the hotels. I was afraid for my life. Obviously I had overreacted. I saw a Pagan or a Warlock on every motorcycle when there were obviously doctors, lawyers and everyman. I think my reaction was caused by the first case I encountered while I was interning at a criminal law firm my second summer of law school. It was the first preliminary hearing I had ever attended. A young woman had been brutally raped by a gang of Pagans. The firm I worked with represented one of them. The woman, who was in her early twenties, had been savagely beaten with pots, pans and other available domestic objects. The photos of the bruised, black-and-blue woman were impossible to look at, the psychological scars impossible to fathom.

We kept driving. We passed through Saratoga Springs. More motorcycles. No available hotel room. Several miles outside Ballston Spa the number of motorcycles began to dwindle. Then there was an occasional motorcycle and finally none. I heaved a sigh of relief. We had to change our vacation plans, to a place far away from the motorcycle convention. We looked at the map. It was June 10, the anniversary of my father's death according to the Jewish calendar. The anniversary is called *Yahrtzeit* in Hebrew. Usually *Yahrtzeit* is commemorated by lighting a candle and saying a prayer. And then I saw something on the map—Cooperstown, the home of the Baseball Hall of Fame. It was a little out of the way, but I told John I wanted to go because it was a fitting way to memorialize my dad, much better than lighting a measly candle, saying a prayer or even visiting his grave.

My dad was a warm, quiet man who was willing to help anyone he met. He ventured out with a topcoat over his pajamas at four in the morning in a snowstorm to make sure a sick child got her medicine. He had a divine patience in explaining in painstaking detail why a doctor had prescribed a certain medication. He allowed grace period after grace period when he knew a family couldn't afford to pay an outstanding balance. He loved children. They would take to him immediately. He would get down on the floor and play with them, including me, whenever he could. As much as he loved children, he loved baseball, although his hectic schedule, an average of eighty hours a week laboring in the drugstore, didn't allow him much time to watch his favorite sport. He never got to Cooperstown, although he always wanted to go.

For as long as I can remember my father had a small black mole on his right temple. When I was in my first year in law school it suddenly began to get larger. My mother persuaded my father to see a doctor about it. The doctor referred him to a surgeon. The surgeon, who was the brother-in-law of my mother's closest friend, removed the mole and told my mother the bad news. It was a melanoma, a virulent kind of cancer. A death sentence. My mother didn't want to upset my father or me and told us it was nothing, a basal cell cancer that wouldn't recur. I always wondered if my father would have lived his life differently if he had known about his death sentence.

Around the same time my father had the mole removed and my mother received his death sentence, I visited a friend who was a first-year medical student. She happened to be studying skin cancer at the time. I looked at the photos in her textbook. "My dad's mole looks exactly like that one," I said, pointing to a photo. "What is it?"

"It's called melanoma and if anyone has it, it's curtains."

I had always lived in fear of my father's death. I knew if my father died I would be left alone with my mother.

As soon as I got home I called my mother, "Does daddy have melanoma?"

"Why?"

I told her what my friend had said about melanoma and its being "curtains."

"What did she mean by curtains?"

"That it would be fatal. Why are you asking me that? I thought you said it was basal cell." I don't think she answered me.

For the next year or so my dad seemed fine, although one day he drove off the road. I speculated that he had been tired after a long day of work. He had never been a great driver. Early in their marriage, along with ceding control of just about everything else, my father let my mother drive most of the time.

In 1973 my father decided to close the store for good, not altogether voluntarily. Discount drugstores were arriving on the scene. A Rite Aid moved in right around the corner and many of my father's customers, in spite of the early morning deliveries and the patient explanations, opted for Rite Aid's lower prices. Then the discount chain offered to buy out my father for a pittance. They also wanted him to work for them part-time. He agreed to both proposals. He thought that selling was a better idea than just letting the business that he and my mother had nurtured for twenty-five years founder and die. My mother likely encouraged my father's retirement because she knew of his secret death sentence.

Right after they sold the business my parents went to Hawaii for a vacation. It was their twenty-sixth anniversary. I sent them a flower bouquet that was delivered to their room. The last photo I have of my father is of him standing in the Hawaii hotel room, holding the flower arrangement, a warm smile on his face.

When my parents got back from their vacation, I noticed a change in my father. Although Sam's Rite Aid work schedule was far less rigorous than the one he was used to, he was constantly tired. I blamed my mother for encouraging him to close the store. He needed the spark of working longer hours, I thought. I remembered anecdotes my parents would tell about their friends who had retired early and promptly died.

I came to visit my father on his sixty-third birthday, May 17, 1973. I hadn't seen my dad since early April. I was busy tying up loose ends in my last year of law school and dating my Southern Baptist law professor. My father was limping. He slurred his words. He was almost completely deaf. A childhood disease had destroyed the hearing in his left ear. Now his right ear was going. I proudly presented him with tickets to a Phillies game scheduled for the middle of June. "Thanks, Joanie," he said weakly, as he kissed me. I wondered if he would be able to hear the crack of the bat at the game. Although it would have been apparent to almost anyone that a serious neurological problem was becoming rapidly worse, my mother and I decided to address only the hearing deficit.

Several days later my mother brought my father to an eminent ear, nose and throat specialist in Center City Philadelphia. I met them at the doctor's office. What had become of my father in the last few days? Suddenly he was a shuffling, feeble old man with a white puff of hair surrounding his bald spot. I could see the alarm in the doctor's eyes: "Take him to Temple Hospital immediately."

Once my father arrived at the emergency room, he deteriorated even more. They thought at first that he had had a stroke. My father's hearing loss didn't concern the doctors at the hospital. Whether my father would live or die was what they worried about. My mother was trying to make my father more comfortable in his hospital bed, when he let fly at her a string of expletives. I had never heard my father curse at anyone, let alone my mother, and in the midst of the demise of my father's brain, there was some gallows humor. "Shit, Rose, what the fuck are you doing?" he yelled. He had rarely raised his voice to her. I decided that this finally was my father's revenge. He had stored up all of these epithets in a corner of his brain to retaliate for my mother's forcing him out of the liquor store business with its forty-hour weeks, putting him in an eighty-hour-a-week job and dooming any possibility of leisure time to follow his beloved baseball. He had never had the guts to lodge all these complaints or shout obscenities at my mother when he was lucid. She was too formidable. But now my father was loosing all those curses at her, words he had been too kind or too afraid to say before.

Soon after my father was admitted to the hospital, he was transferred to Intensive Care. My mother told the doctors, "He had a melanoma on his face."

"We don't think that has anything to do with what is wrong with him now."

I overheard her conversation with the doctors and I was shocked. "You told me it was basal cell, nothing."

"You know he couldn't have handled that. He is such a sensitive person. He would have been so nervous he wouldn't have been able to live his life."

"Why did you lie to me?"

"I didn't want you to worry."

When I first visited my father in Intensive Care, I wasn't sure he knew I was there. He was making imaginary capsules, hundreds of them. So, this is the way pharmacists go crazy, I thought. He scooped imaginary powder with one side of the capsule and put the top on. Then he went on to the next capsule. Seeing him this way was both comforting and alarming. He seemed so calm and happy, doing what he had done for much of his life. I remembered all of the afternoons I spent in the store. He would show me how to make capsules so I could stay alongside him and make my own play capsules while he made real ones. He always wanted me to somehow follow in his footsteps, not to be a pharmacist but something better, like a toxicologist. But now he would have no more ambitions for either himself or me. All I could think of was that line from Hamlet, "O, what a noble mind is here o'erthrown!" I was convinced that my amazingly stable father had become unglued and was now psychotic. "Bring in a psychiatrist," I pleaded. The doctors didn't respond. They looked at me in a pitying, condescending way. They knew this was an organic brain disease; they just weren't sure of the exact diagnosis. They ordered test after test.

In 1973 there was not much in the way of noninvasive brain testing. The neurosurgeon suggested an arteriogram, which involved shooting dye into arteries in the neck to visualize the arteries in the brain to see if there was a clot or some other kind of obstruction. When my father came back from the test he seemed worse than before. He looked as if he had been in a war with the diagnostic medical establishment. There was bright pink dye all over his neck and pink tinges on his pure white hair. The arteriogram showed nothing. Still, the doctors ignored my mother's concerns about melanoma.

My father was moved back and forth between Intensive Care and a conventional room, although there seemed to be little progress and there was certainly no diagnosis. Now and then I could see a glimmer of my dad's old self and then he would regress to what I thought was his crazed pharmacist psychosis.

Then it was time for my graduation from law school. The person who would have been most proud of my accomplishments could not be there. He was the one who gloried in my academic achievements and cared little that I wasn't perfectly coiffed or married. After graduation I went to see my father in his hospital room. I was wearing the baby blue piqué dress I had chosen for graduation. We were spared caps and gowns and in true 1970s fashion were encouraged to wear whatever we wanted. "Daddy, I graduated." I showed my father my diploma. He smiled at me. I wasn't sure he really understood. My mother was lukewarm about my graduation. All she wanted me to do was get my picture in the engagements section of the *Jewish Exponent*. I already had a taste of what life was going to be like without my father in my corner. I kept that blue gown for twenty-five years. I couldn't bear to give it away, not because I had worn it to law school graduation but because my father had touched the sleeve of the dress as I kissed him on the cheek and showed him my diploma.

The day after my graduation my father was back in Intensive Care, busy making his capsules. The doctors were still stumped about my father's diagnosis. But he gave them a way out. He had a massive heart attack. All of the invasive procedures had to stop. He was taken to Cardiac Intensive Care, this time he was unconscious. Now he seemed not to be there at all anymore. No more imaginary prescriptions were being filled. My little daddy, as I used to call him because by the time I was twelve I was taller than he, was gone. I couldn't bear to see him like that.

After the heart attack, I stayed with my mother. We both needed emotional support and both of us were accustomed to getting that support from my father. He wasn't there to give it, so we had to make do with each other. On a Tuesday morning, June 12, the phone rang. I answered it. It was the neurosurgeon. "Please come to the hospital immediately." My mother and I dawdled. It took us an inordinate amount of time to get dressed. We ate breakfast. Hours after the morning phone call we finally got to the hospital. The bed where my father had been was empty, the sheets stripped off, the mattress folded over. My father had already died. I felt guilty that I hadn't been there to hold his hand. Neither my mother nor I could face the fact that my father was dying. We both had known why we had been summoned to the hospital but we couldn't handle it so we procrastinated, hoping that by the time we got there everything would be okay. It was far from okay. As we stood by the empty bed, a nurse came in to put on new sheets. They were such a bright white, they hurt my eyes. And where my father had been, at least in body the day before, there was no one. The nurse left. The neurosurgeon came into the room with the empty bed. He was surprised we hadn't arrived sooner. He said that my father had never come out of the coma and passed away peacefully and, though he didn't say it, alone. He tried to comfort us, which was a good thing because after years of all-out warfare, neither of us was any good at comforting the other.

We left the hospital and returned to my mother's deafeningly quiet apartment. With tears streaming down my cheeks I rummaged through my father's drawers to find the Phillies tickets I had given him on his birthday. I found them. The game was scheduled for the next week. I threw the tickets into the trash.

At the doctor's request we reluctantly consented to an autopsy. We wanted to know what had killed our sweet Sam. Weeks later the doctor called with the autopsy results. "It was melanoma. His brain looked like a raisin bread." I imagined the raisins to be small black melanoma tumors that had consumed my father's brain. I could never bring myself to ask if I was right.

Whatever religious faith I had, and there wasn't much left after being force-fed religious school for fourteen years, was lost. It was difficult for me to believe in a God who had made such a good man endure so much suffering. I'm sure that somewhere there is a Talmudic answer. I wasn't interested in hearing it.

My mother spent years lamenting the fact that had my father not had a heart attack, she could have taken care of him in his last cancer-ridden three to six months. I was glad that his suffering had ended with the heart attack.

Hundreds of people came to my father's funeral to say goodbye to the man who had brought them prescriptions in the middle of the night, who reassured them about their diseases, and who always greeted them with a warm smile and a kind heart. And then, as is Jewish tradition, after we buried my father, people came back to my mother's apartment for lunch. My father always decried what he called "those parties." He always thought it was inappropriate for people to eat, drink booze and laugh so soon after a funeral. And there they were noshing, drinking and laughing after his funeral too. He would have hated that.

The requisite *shiva* happened. For three days after the funeral people came to pay their respects. My Southern Baptist boyfriend at the time came to pay his respects to my mother and me. I was continuing the tradition that I began in first grade with Tommy of never picking a Jewish guy. This was the first time since Tommy that I introduced one of my non-Jewish boyfriends to my mother. I usually kept them carefully under wraps. The *shiva*-sitting Southern Baptist appeared in spanking new clothes and shoes. And then my mother did something I had never seen her do. She cut him dead. She didn't give him the time of day. I was appalled and embarrassed but didn't have the energy to argue with her.

I had enough to worry about. My relationship with the Southern Baptist was unraveling. He had found himself a *shiksa* while I was busy with my father's illness. The bar exam was only six weeks away and I had not yet begin to study. I was in the stupor of grief. My law school friends saw my condition, told me exactly what I needed to know for the exam and got me through. I memorized like a zombie, "Murder is the unlawful killing of another with malice." I didn't even stop to think what a lawful killing would look like or what exactly malice was. Somehow I passed the bar. It was no mean feat under any circumstance but under the circumstances I had just endured it was nothing short of miraculous. When I called my mother to tell her, she said, with no enthusiasm at all, "That's nice." I missed my father more than usual that day.

By the time John and I were deciding where to go in upstate New York that June day, my father had been dead for twenty-two years. I thought that Cooperstown would be the perfect place not just to honor my father's memory, but also to celebrate his life. I had pictured Cooperstown as the Baseball Hall of Fame flanked on each side by seedy motels. I was wrong. We passed a pristine lake on the way into the baseball town. I wasn't prepared for an eighteenth-century colonial town that had at its center a tasteful brick building that housed the Hall of Fame. To the right of the Hall was a baseball diamond where teams from all over the country came to play. While we were there, so was a team called the Black Sox, which reminded us of the White Sox scandal in the early part of the twentieth century. The White Sox were renamed the Black Sox because they were caught gambling on baseball. The scandal brought down baseball great Shoeless Joe Jackson and provided a storyline for John Sayles's movie *Eight Men Out*. We had a picture taken handing the Black Sox money. The better picture was a photo taken of John and me, the most touristy photo either of us had ever had taken. We each donned baseball outfits: John a Toronto Blue Jays uniform, me a Phillies outfit. I was holding a baseball glove, John a bat.

The baseball museum itself was the perfect place to remember my dad. I felt as if he was there with us. I choked up when I walked into the main hall where bronze plaques commemorate each member. There they were, the Phillies I had watched with my dad at Connie Mack—Richie Ashburn, Robin Roberts. My father's favorites, the Jewish contingent, had made it too—Hank Greenberg and Sandy Koufax. I think that Greenberg and Koufax made my dad think he could have been a great ballplayer too if he hadn't had the responsibility to support a succession of families— his parents, because his dad, a tailor and union organizer, couldn't make ends meet, and then my mother and me.

I felt that our visit to the Baseball Hall of Fame was the best tribute I could have paid to my father. Baseball was his escape from his lifetime of grueling work. He had shared that pastime with me. Now I was seeing the Hall of Fame he never had the time to visit. His spirit was there with me in a place he would have adored.

THE GIRL WITH THE HAT HANGS ON

Things with John and The Girl with the Hat weren't exactly over. They were still hanging on to each other for dear life, albeit platonically, much to my consternation. Call me old fashioned, but I was a woman who always thought a man should have only one girlfriend at a time, even if the second one was otherwise occupied with a girlfriend of her own. I asked John to cut off contact with The Girl with the Hat. He wouldn't. It became a cause of friction between us.

It came to a head for me that first summer we spent together in Philadelphia. I had a teaching gig in Newark. I taught trial skills to fledgling lawyers. John decided to come along so he could spend time in New York with the girls with the hats. All of them went to Lincoln Center for an outdoor *klezmer* music concert. At one point the original girl with the hat asked John, as he related to me later, "Does it bother Joan that you're spending time with me?"

"Yes," John told me he answered.

Apparently The Girl with the Hat and her ex-boyfriend didn't really care that their seeing each other and continuing a friendship troubled me. John was a man and did what he felt like. But wasn't The Girl with the Hat supposedly a feminist who should have had some empathy for the woman who took her place? John and The Girl with the Hat continued to be in touch with each other, perhaps for a longer time than they would have had I not objected so much.

MY THIRTY-FIVE-DOLLAR ENGAGEMENT RING

After John's first summer in Philadelphia and an autumn of our jetting back and forth between Toronto and Philadelphia, John came to visit me in January 1996. We went shopping for my Valentine present. We wandered into a jewelry store on Pine Street and chose a marcasite ring. The ring cost thirty-five dollars, including the charge for sizing. It wouldn't be ready for a few days. The storeowner assured me that I could pick it up before Valentine's Day. I would be alone when I picked it up. John would be back in Toronto.

When we left the store and began walking back to my house, John said, "How about if that's our engagement ring?"

"Okay," I answered.

Somehow I expected a more romantic proposal. Must have been all of those articles in the *New York Times* Styles Section cataloguing romantic proposal after romantic proposal everywhere from the Eiffel Tower to the Taj Mahal. Shouldn't we have gone to an elegant restaurant? Wasn't a sparkling diamond supposed to be hidden inside a chocolate éclair? Wasn't John supposed to get down on his knees and ask for my hand in marriage? Shouldn't there be the sound of violins swelling in the background?

But I was forty-eight and at last on my way to the altar. How picky can a girl be? My engagement didn't happen the way I or my mother or any of those betrothed girls in the *Jewish Exponent* would have imagined it. My mother wouldn't have wanted me to settle for anything less than a one-carat fine diamond from Kellmer's, the jewelry store where my father bought her a three-carat rock on their tenth anniversary. I settled for a ring that was less than she had dreamed of, but the guy who gave it to me, even though he appeared later than I had hoped, was just right.

THE NO PROTEIN DIET

When I returned to Toronto with my engagement ring in the spring, I was browsing in the University of Toronto Bookstore while John went to fetch a journal in the library. I looked up and there on a table right in front of me was a book with a bright white cover and red letters, *The Kidney Patient's Handbook.* I looked through the book briefly and then I showed it to John when he met me later at the bookstore. "I found a book. It was the first thing I saw when I walked into the store. It says there's a way to prevent dialysis." John looked at the blurb on the dustcover. He looked relieved and said, "Let's buy it."

I thought that the book's being right under my nose was an omen. It touted a very low-protein diet to slow the progress to dialysis. The diet was advocated by Mackenzie Walser, a physician at Johns Hopkins Medical Center in Baltimore. This wasn't the low-protein diet John had followed for years. This diet was much more strict. It allowed almost no protein.

John decided to make an appointment to see Dr. Walser, since his kidney function was steadily declining and the doctors he saw in Canada had no solutions. It was suspected that John had glomerular nephritis, a disease where the glomeruli, the kidney's tiny filters, shut down and stop straining toxins from the blood. The diagnosis was not assured because a biopsy done in Canada that would have shown the disease was inconclusive. I kept thinking that the diagnosis was wrong because John had a host of symptoms. I thought that all of the symptoms pointed to something more systemic than kidney disease. He had glaucoma, high blood pressure, depression, huge hematomas. I thought that some smart doctor could put it all together and find that he actually had some other illness that was curable by a magic pill. I gathered all of John's medical records and gave them to the smartest internist I knew in Philadelphia and he came up with nothing different from what all of the Canadian doctors had said. John was suffering from kidney disease, my doctor friend told me, and in time his kidneys would shut down and he would need dialysis or a transplant. No one could predict exactly when John's kidneys would fail but eventually they would.

John walked around with a sword suspended precariously over his head. He was always waiting for the other shoe to drop. Sadly, he wasted much of the present agonizing about what the future would bring. He had a hard time not obsessing about his health. He had come by the obsession about his health honestly. His mother had been sick most of the time he was growing up. She had psoriasis, which was a constant source of itching, pain and embarrassment. The disease prevented her from doing any household chores that required her to put her hands in water— most household chores. She was on a steady diet of uppers and tranquilizers. When he was young and his dad was on the road, John would often find his mom passed out on the bathroom floor. He had to help her to bed without any adult help. He constantly worried about his mother's health, a precursor to his later worrying about his own.

A few weeks after discovering *The Kidney Patient's Handbook* we were in Dr. Walser's office. He explained that he was doing research on the diet we had read about in the book. John agreed to be a guinea pig. Dr. Walser tested John's kidneys and offered him what I always called the "No Protein Diet" supplemented with amino acids. At first the diet was a real challenge for both of us, for John because he could eat so few things, and for me who carefully shopped for the few things he could eat. Almost everything has protein, even foods you would least expect, like bread. John had to bake his own special low protein bread. He could eat fruits, berries and vegetables. Not nuts, seeds or tofu like most self-respecting vegetarians because they were full of protein. After the novelty and challenge of the diet wore off it faded into sheer boredom. For some the boredom of food would not have been a big deal, but John loved to eat and he loved to cook. He persevered with the diet, hoping for a one or two year reprieve from dialysis. Dialysis was so frightening to John that he refused to learn about it. He just imagined it to be as bad as it could possibly be, years of being tied to a machine for five hours three times a week, a machine that would help him live by acting as an artificial kidney but that might cause a host of other life-threatening illnesses.

John had to see Dr. Walser in Baltimore every few months so I rarely went to Toronto, which made me very happy. I had grown no fonder of the city. It didn't matter how many times I went. I was always relieved to get back to Philadelphia.

Once John began to go to Johns Hopkins I accompanied him. It was the first time I realized how sick he was and how frightening each trip to the doctor was for him. The kidney disease John had was a silent killer. At the beginning it had few apparent symptoms. There were no visible signs, no discomfort. John looked as if nothing was wrong with him when we first saw Dr. Walser. He had bouts of fatigue and could do less strenuous exercise than he had in the past. You couldn't know he was sick by just looking at him. His complexion was less ruddy than it had been when I first met him, but basically he looked fine. Sometimes when he complained it was difficult to be sympathetic because he looked so healthy. When I went with him to Johns Hopkins I realized how serious his illness was.

We would arrive early in the morning for a test that measured the glomerular filtration rate (GFR) of the kidneys, which assessed the kidney function. A radioactive dye was injected and blood and urine were taken at half-hour intervals. The testing process lasted hours and then we had the long wait for the results.

John was willing to do anything to avoid kidney failure. He was always very compliant with medication so he assumed he could handle a very strict diet too. What he hadn't factored into his acceptance of a severely restricted diet was his love of food. He is a very talented cook, a creative one. He learned cooking at his father's knee. His mother couldn't cook because of her psoriasis so when his father was home, his father did all the family cooking. John loved to eat, at home, in restaurants, everywhere. Since he had to restrict his protein intake a few years before, he thought about food all the time. Sometimes he dreamed about it. Leaving food behind was difficult.

John was always on edge when he saw Dr. Walser. The first test results from Johns Hopkins were not good. John's kidney function was worse than the last time it had been tested in Canada. The sword of dialysis was lowering over John's head. I now understood, having seen the test results in black and white, that he wasn't as healthy as he looked. The bad news gave John more motivation to stick to the diet.

I contacted dietitians at Philadelphia hospitals for recipes. I combed the supermarket for foods that had the least protein possible. Our meals became more and more simple, more and more tasteless. John was sad. He missed the foods he loved—cheeseburgers, brisket, cheese steaks, a favorite Philadelphia concoction of strip steak, provolone and fried onions, and White House subs piled high with Italian lunchmeats and cheeses.

We went to the doctor at Johns Hopkins every few months for more than a year. Each time John had to endure the several hour GFR test. He nervously paced the halls of Johns Hopkins waiting for the results. Each time John's kidney function was a little worse. He continued with the diet in the hope that his kidney function would decline at a slower rate, but there was no way to know if that was happening. I admired John's courage in facing his illness and in doing everything he could to get better, even if it meant that all he could eat was the tasteless bread he made himself, fruits and vegetables.

While we were seeing Dr. Walser, the school where John taught for more than thirty years, York University, began to offer early retirement plans. We saw a way for John to move to the United States permanently. He would retire early and leave Toronto. I never really entertained the idea of moving to Canada. I was an American and couldn't see myself anywhere else. The worst experience had been one Thanksgiving that John and I spent in Toronto with a bunch of former and wannabe Americans at a restaurant that served up dried out turkey with small mounds of stuffing and mashed potatoes. It just wasn't the same as the bountiful Thanksgiving dinners I had always enjoyed at home. And I couldn't practice law in Canada. My being a lawyer cut off the Canada versus U.S. debate. The United States it was. John longed to come home to the States. He had never really felt at home in Canada even though he had lived there longer than he had in Cincinnati.

We began to think about making a life for ourselves in Philadelphia. We even began the several-years'-long quest for a house. We weren't sure whether we wanted to be in Philadelphia or the suburbs. We looked for a while in the suburbs, but no house there seemed quite right. On the main arteries in the western suburbs there seemed to be more traffic than there was in Center City Philadelphia. My friends kept telling me that they thought of me as a city girl and they couldn't see me in the suburbs. I tended to agree and realized that I couldn't see John in the suburbs either. I had lived in downtown Philadelphia since graduating from college in 1969. John had lived for years in a Greek area of Toronto called The Danforth. Both of our neighborhoods were lively and had restaurants, shops and supermarkets within steps of our houses.

We started to listen to our friends and began to look for a house in Center City Philadelphia. John's requirement for a quiet place was the most difficult to satisfy.

RELIGION IS THE OPIATE
OF THE SINGLE DIVORCED MAN

In every relationship there are tests. The smarter the partner the more formidable the tests. The smarter the partner the better he is at finding, whether consciously or unconsciously, the chink in his partner's armor, her Achilles' heel. I was not much of a fan of religion, and no fan of any kind of discrimination, no matter what its justification. John rediscovered religion about six months before he was scheduled to move to Philadelphia. A group of Orthodox Jews came after him—he was "the *Minyan* Man," the tenth man they needed to conduct an official prayer session. If you have only nine men it isn't official. And not only was John a man who had been circumcised and *Bar Mitzvahed,* which would have been enough, as the old Passover Song *Dayenu* goes, but he was also a *Kohane,* the most holy of Jews descended from the rabbis who presided at the first temple, descended from Moses' brother Aaron. Hallelujah!

John hadn't had much in the way of Jewish education, just barely enough to be *Bar Mitzvahed*. John had warm memories of his grandfather's enveloping him, Jerry Rubin and his other cousins in a huge shawl at *Yom Kippur* services at an Orthodox *schul*.

John was attracted to this group of Orthodox Jews because he was lonely in Toronto and because he was worried about his health. He thought that the prayers they said for him in synagogue helped him to feel better, although he knew prayers would not cure kidney failure. He also thought that the other members of the *minyan* would take care of him if he became ill during his last several months in Toronto.

Over the next few months John told me more about the group of people he was spending time with. They didn't believe, in true Orthodox fashion, that men and women should pray together. They had to pray separately, first in different rooms in one of the member's houses and later in their makeshift synagogue above a store, a sheet hung between the men and women. In a more established Orthodox synagogue the men would be down in front, the women relegated to a balcony behind them. With this Orthodox infatuation John pushed my discrimination button.

This separation of the sexes reminded me of a time in the middle of the 1960s struggle for civil rights when Rap Brown, a leader in the then-new Black Power Movement, came to speak at my alma mater, the University of Pittsburgh. The speech was held at the Student Union and I scrambled over early to get a good seat. I headed straight for the front of the room. I always liked to sit up close. Brown's ushers were there, held me back and said, "You have to sit in the back. Sit in the back." Since I was no Rosa Parks, I obeyed these formidable-looking black men—that's what we called them then—with their large Afros.

By the time the program started, all of the African Americans in the audience were sitting right up front; the Caucasians were in the back. The back of the auditorium, the back of the bus. I remember nothing Brown said, nothing. I was preoccupied with feeling for the first time like a second-class citizen. I never forgot the feeling of being told where to sit and being separate and unequal. I vowed right then to never allow that kind of second-class citizenship to exist if there were any way to prevent it. I promised myself I would never tolerate anyone forcing me or anyone else to the back of the bus again.

So now, years later, there he was, the man I loved, being part of a group that dictated where I was allowed to sit. Now none of this religious sexism would have been a surprise to me had I hooked my star to what we had called in the 1970s a "male chauvinist pig." But I hadn't, or at least I thought I hadn't. John was the most supportive man I had ever met. He thought it was wonderful that I was a lawyer, even better that I was smart and outspoken. So it came as quite a blow that he suddenly thought it was okay for me to be treated differently from a man. "You don't understand," he said, in one of our heated discussions.

"You're wrong. I do."

"No, you don't. It's just about honoring tradition."

"Bullshit! That's the way that slavery and second class citizenship, whether it be for African Americans or women, has always been justified. They always say 'It's just honoring tradition. It's always been that way.'"

"It's not the same. We're not discriminating against anyone."

"You're discriminating against women. You're discriminating against me."

"But you don't even want to pray."

"That's not the point."

In 1970, the year I entered law school, the Women's Movement, although rampant in colleges, had not yet filtered down to the trade school level. My class at Rutgers was 160 strong. Only eight of us were women. Six women sat obsequiously on the right side of the third row in every class, in what was known as "chick row." I sat on the left side of the class with the hippies. Towards the back was Liz, the sole African American woman, who sat with the other black students. One of the first things I noticed was that the professors referred to the class collectively as "Gentlemen." What about us, Liz, the six chicks and me? Armed with my lessons from Germaine Greer and Betty Friedan, I approached each professor in turn and told him I was offended by being excluded. Slowly they started calling us "Ladies and Gentlemen," a small victory but something. I would point out chauvinism whenever I saw it and likely made quite a name for myself among the faculty.

I struggled with the legal curriculum in my first semester. It was far more concrete than I thought it would be and required more memorization than I was used to. I was frustrated by the lack of any conceptual discussions.

I finally summoned up the nerve to ask one of my more approachable teachers, "When are we were going to talk about justice?"

He said, "We don't talk about justice here."

Then I knew I was really in trouble.

A few months into the term, having recovered from a heavy dose of law school brainwashing, I figured out the real game some of the professors were playing with the women in our class. In Civil Procedure we regularly were forced to present a case, an ego-deflating process where the student stands, recites the facts, what the court decided and why, only to have the professor ask a lot of questions until the victim called on answers incorrectly. The method was named after Socrates. The sadistic practice of his method by lesser minds must regularly make that master teacher revolve in his grave. My turn inevitably came. My professor, who had Frankenstein's monster's grace and manner, called on me. I stood up and as I was reciting, I realized that I had the court's reasoning all wrong. "You have the facts wrong," the professor said.

"The facts weren't wrong; it was the reasoning,." I countered.

He ignored me. Why spend valuable time on some uppity woman who should have been home doing laundry? This kind of benign neglect, an affront far worse than exclusion by word choice, happened repeatedly to Liz, the six chicks and me.

First-year finals were approaching, a trial for any law student. For me it was especially difficult. I had never had to memorize so many seemingly irrelevant facts. I worried as finals approached. I always worried about finals and cried what my father called "wolf" about probably getting a C or flunking. I never got worse than a B in college, except for that pesky C in logic, which should have been fair warning that maybe law should not have been my career of choice. This time I was really worried.

I hadn't realized that my lobbying for equal treatment had come to the attention of the patrician dean. A few days before my finals, examinations that strike fear in even the most confident law student's heart, the dean greeted me. I was slouched on a rickety wooden chair in the hallway outside of the professors' offices, wearing some version of the frayed bell-bottom jeans and navy blue turtleneck without benefit of bra that I wore every day in my first semester, my Frye boots propped up on a coffee table. I sat up straight when I saw the dean. I took my boots off the table. "I have been watching you, Miss Saltzman," he said peering down at me over his half glasses, "I believe you are going to fail all of your finals." I opened my mouth but I couldn't speak. He left. I had never flunked anything. Not even art in high school. Miss Richardson let me squeak by with a D. I was shaken but also challenged. I decided that I would not fail my finals no matter what I had to do. I didn't. The dean never spoke to me again.

I figured I had suffered my share of discrimination on the basis of sex in law school, where many of my professors thought my mind would be better-used planning dinner parties than tackling the nuances of the law. I wasn't going to go to any synagogue where I couldn't read from the Torah if I wanted to or sit wherever I damn well pleased.

I had had my share of religion and religious education—beginning when I was four and ending at eighteen. I might have left religious school earlier but I kept winning scholarships, and in my family it was a sin to turn down a scholarship. I finally ended my Jewish education soon after I discovered cosmology and got no good answers reconciling that cogent theory with Genesis. I grew up in a Conservative synagogue and prayed every *Shabbat, Rosh Hashanah* and *Yom Kippur* when I lived at home. Once I left home I decided that I didn't want to attend synagogue any more, and survived a shaky year when I worried about my mortality because I had shunned the holidays when God supposedly decided who would live or die. Religion had never been a balm to me as it had been to other people I knew. I wasn't sure if there was a God. If someday I decided that there was one, I could pray to Him or Her without the trappings of organized religion. I was glad that I was Jewish and preferred to live my life as a secular Jew rather than within the dictates of a particular synagogue. I figured that the best part of being Jewish was that if I wanted to pray I didn't need to go to a house of worship. I could pray at home. If I didn't want to pray on a regular basis, that was okay too. The rules weren't that strict, unless you were Orthodox or Conservative.

Now the man I loved was a born-again Orthodox Jew. There had been a number of stumbling blocks in John's and my path. This one was a huge boulder. John told me about the rebirth of his spirituality, about how much the people cared for him, prayed for him, fed him and asked him for money. On the rare occasions that I visited him, I refused to be a second-class citizen in the synagogue. I never went to services there. We argued about religion. We fought about it. I wondered if he respected me as a person if he thought I was unfit to read from the Torah or sit next to him when he prayed. Then it dawned on me. Why was I asking for equality? I didn't even want to pray. The battle was joined and suddenly I realized it wasn't so much a spiritual awakening as it was a battle for its own sake. We each wanted to drive a wedge between us so we wouldn't have to take that big scary step toward marriage.

In March 1997 I finally relented. I agreed to go with John to the synagogue leader's house. I understood immediately why John loved the home-cooked vegetarian food prepared by the leader's mother and sister, both accomplished women relegated to the kitchen to prepare food for the men. And then there was the leader's wife, a much younger woman who had already delivered the first of what they hoped would be many children but alas it was a girl. Had she really been the perfect Orthodox wife she would have had a boy, so eventually he could be a first-class citizen, read the Torah and pray with the men. Although the young mother was beautiful, she looked worn out for her twenty-some years. She wore a dowdy long dress and a babushka. I didn't think I would ever use the word "babushka"—my mother used it to describe the kerchiefs tied around the heads of the older Russian-born women at our synagogue. The Orthodox wife did the blessing over the candles, a prayer that women are allowed to make in the company of men. When it came time for the more serious Friday night praying, the men went into the next room, presumably so that the women wouldn't distract them.

When the services were over we met John's son, Jesse, who I hoped would be my ally in all of this. We went to the home of another man in the *minyan* for *Shabbat* dinner. We drove. The man and his wife walked. Orthodox Jews are not allowed to drive, use money, operate machinery or even turn lights on and off on the Sabbath. It was that night that I met Brent, another member of the congregation. Brent had a brother who was suffering from diabetes and kidney failure. Brent was thinking of giving his brother a kidney. What a selfless but perhaps foolish thing to do, I thought. What if he needed the kidney later?

Brent, Jesse, John and I arrived at our *Shabbat* dinner date. When we entered the house we realized that there was a problem. Ordinarily in Orthodox families lights will be left on in the house before *Shabbat* so that there is no necessity to turn them off and on during the Sabbath. Our hosts had forgotten to leave the lights on in the kitchen and the bathroom. The woman of the house had to grope her way into the kitchen to retrieve the food and we all had to go to the bathroom in the dark. The wife seemed to handle the problem with the dark kitchen in stride, which led me to believe that it had happened to her before. I told John quietly that I would volunteer to be what is called the *Shabbat Goy,* usually a gentile who turns the lights on when Orthodox or Conservative Jews can't. John told me not to offer because it would be a sin for me to do it or for them to let me, since I wasn't really a *goy,* just a second-class Jew. We all made do with the darkness. And then it happened. After a series of prayers the man of the house started breaking the traditional braided egg bread called *challah.* Then before we knew it he began quickly and without any warning heaving chunks of the bread down the table to anyone who could catch them. Now I had had lots of Jewish education and had participated in the celebration of many Jewish festivals but I had never seen anything like this before. Maybe it was a Canadian Orthodox custom. I had to duck a few times to avoid being beaned by the flying bread. I avoided looking at John or Jesse. I just looked down. I felt those giggles rising up, the twelve-year-old girl ones that plagued me during High Holiday services when I sat with my preteen friends, but managed to suppress them until John, Jesse and I got outside. Then I didn't know whether to laugh or cry. "How can you be with these people? Jesse, give me a hand here." After all he majored in Comparative Religion and was about to go off to the London School of Economics to study cults and new religions.

"Dad, these people really believe in God, not as an idea but as something that really exits and controls everything."

"No, they don't. Do they? They have been so nice to me."

"They do. They think that God really exists and has control over what happens. They don't think of God as a concept."

When John was leaving Toronto for Philadelphia, the synagogue decided to have a party to say goodbye to him. I refused to go to the services that preceded the party. No way I was sitting on the other side of the *mehitza,* in the back of the bus. All I could think as I looked around at the beatific faces at the farewell lunch was that we were lucky to be leaving before John fell further under their spell.

prenuptial

By the spring of 1997, John and I had seen the inside of about a quarter of the Center City Philadelphia housing stock east of Broad Street. Time was running out. John was scheduled to move to Philadelphia in May. It seemed as if we were looking for the impossible, an affordable house in pristine condition on a quiet street with a garden and a parking space that didn't have a kitchen in the basement.

We knew we would have to give up something. Finally our realtor told us she knew of a house that was about to come on the market that had most of what we were looking for, except for the pristine condition. By the time we saw the house, we were beaten down. We had just a few weeks before John moved to Philadelphia and in spite of two years of tramping through houses, we had found nothing. The house our realtor showed us had beautiful architectural details, especially a circa 1880s bell on the second floor attached to a brass knob next to the front door. John always said, "We bought the bell and the house came with it." The house smelled like cat pee when we entered. Since both of us had cats, we weren't as turned off by the cat pee smell as others might have been. The home's current occupants had an elderly cat, likely too senile to hit the litter box. The kitchen had to be redone. The floors had to be refinished. A paint job was necessary. All of this was much more than we had bargained for, but time was getting short and we didn't have much choice. And so we signed an Agreement of Sale. The inspection turned up even more problems. I more than John was taken by the charm of the place and I figured that all of the newfound problems could be handled.

Into the lives of every savvy couple in love, especially when they buy a house together, comes the prenuptial agreement. Neither John nor I doubted the need for one, especially John, who had been divorced twice. Neither of John's marriages resulted in messy financial problems. The first didn't because neither John nor his wife owned anything. John and his second wife were able to divide what they owned without much trouble, although now and then John would say somewhat wistfully, "I used to have a beautiful Baskin print but Judy got it."

I had heard legions of stories about messy divorces that had left two solvent people destitute. My worst nightmare had always been that somehow I would wind up homeless. I actually could imagine myself on the streets of Philadelphia without a roof over my head. The prenuptial was one way to guard against that.

When we signed the Agreement of Sale on our house, I knew it was time to call the lawyers. That's right—lawyers. One lawyer wasn't enough because our interests were different—mine was to preserve what I had, John's was to preserve what he had for himself and Jesse. So each of us had to get a lawyer.

Here we were a lawyer and a college professor in love, but laboring under the stress of a recent Jewish rebirth, packing up two houses, renovating a new one, John's moving back to his native land and tackling a new job, a teaching spot at the University of Pennsylvania that had opened just at the right moment, and adjusting to living together. Now we had to decide how to divide up our money and the house we didn't own yet if we decided to get divorced, and who would get what if either or both of us died.

We and our lawyers wrangled over the clauses in the prenuptial for a few weeks before we arrived at a détente, only days before we were scheduled to tie the knot. Our nerves were frayed. As in all good negotiations, especially ones between only children, neither of us got exactly what we wanted.

THE FIFTY-MINUTE WEDDING PLANNER

For the over-the-hill-marriage set, considerations are different. When my mother carefully placed the *Jewish Exponent* on my bed, always open to the engagement page, she had a lavish wedding in mind.

I had never been a matching napkins, tablecloths and brides-maids kind of girl. I had no interest in a cast of thousands at my wedding, no matter how long I had waited to tie the knot. How many crock-pots, toasters and vases could a couple that had not one but two fully equipped households use? Nor did I want a white dress that cost thousands of dollars. I could never figure out why anyone would spend so much for a dress whose shelf life was at best a few hours.

John and I had the real concerns of lovers who marry late in life. John had to have health insurance as soon as he came to live in Philadelphia. The only way he could get insurance for his steadily decaying kidneys was to marry me and piggyback on to my health plan. Any other plan would have disqualified him because he had a preexisting, medically pricey condition. My plan with the Philadelphia Bar Association had no such exclusion for anyone who married a Bar Association lawyer.

Elkton, Maryland, was the place we chose to get married. We could get a license quickly, without the necessity of blood tests or other formalities that Philadelphia required. Elkton had a resonance for me, not exactly a romantic resonance. When I was in high school in the years before *Rowe v. Wade* and readily accessible abortions, the girls in eleventh or twelfth grade who had the misfortune to become pregnant would, shotgun to their boyfriends' heads or not, skulk south to Elkton to get married. We would watch the belly of the most recently rumored unfortunate grow, only to hear that she and her now-fiancé had an appointment with the Elkton justice of the peace.

We had to go to Maryland a few days before our wedding to get our marriage license. It took only a little over an hour to drive to decrepit downtown Elkton. I had expected a town dedicated to nuptials—a quaint wedding cake bakery, dozens of wedding chapels, and rows of stores to buy something old, new, borrowed or blue. I was wrong. There were almost no marriage-related businesses. There was only a 5&10, a few beer joints and a single storefront chapel. We were likely confronted with the same sad town my high school pals saw when they came to say their much-too-premature "I do's."

I, on the other hand, had come to Elkton for my belated middle-aged nuptials. We applied for the license and received it from a frowning bureaucrat who didn't laugh when John commented, "All you have to do to get married here is to prove that you are over eighteen and not marrying your sister."

She ignored him and said, "Sign here."

I guess she had heard that comment dozens of times before and to her it wasn't funny. You would expect that a place that catered to the joy of young, middle-aged and senior love would have been more joyous, but a job's a job and there was no joy in this Mudville.

It wasn't that there were no choices in Elkton. We had a choice of being married by someone at the marriage license bureau or by someone in the only wedding chapel in town. The privately run chapel was dark, dingy and decidedly Christian. All the quotes in the sample ceremony and on the certificates were from the New Testament. Since we were decidedly Jewish and preferred the Old Testament over the newer one, the chapel just wasn't for us. It was bad enough that we weren't being married by a rabbi and that for years I hadn't gone to *Rosh Hashanah* and *Yom Kippur* services. Being married in a Christian ceremony would have been enough to be stricken down by a Jewish God if there was one. So we scurried back to the justice of the peace to book the courtroom.

We still had no place to hold our wedding luncheon and it was only two days away. The only restaurant in town reeked of beer and cigarettes, so that was out. I wasn't sure where to turn until I noticed that there was a lawyer's office on Elkton's main street. I figured that one of my brother attorneys would know of a decent restaurant in these parts. He said he did and sent us to a place in Chesapeake City, a few miles away. We were in luck. The restaurant looked lovely and had space for twelve of us on short notice.

Our next hurdle was finding the site for the honeymoon. We knew that there were travel agencies designed specifically to pick out wonderful honeymoon destinations. We only had time for a one-day honeymoon because we settled on our house the day after the wedding. We figured we would have to find a place nearby. We drove a few miles past the location for our reception and found at first blush what looked like a lovely bed and breakfast next to a horse farm. We booked it.

We chose May 21 for the wedding both because it was just a few days after John arrived from Canada and because we both figured that John would have less trouble remembering the date since he was born on June 21. We told our friends that we were having a very low-key wedding and that the dress was casual. Both John and I intended to wear tie-dye to commemorate our heydays in the 1960s.

On May 21 we got up early. For some reason, we decided that before we went to Elkton that we would stop at the American Automobile Association to get John's Pennsylvania driver's license. This was particularly odd since John had a year leeway after he moved to Philadelphia to get his license. I put on the tie-dyed dress I had intended to wear (it was actually a bathing suit cover-up that John had bought me) and decided it was all wrong. There had to be something in between a cotton multicolored cover-up and a pricey white dress with a train. I opted for a red and white flowered dress I happened to have in my closet with ruffles here and there. John did stick to the tie-dyed theme. He wore a tie-dyed shirt but put a blazer over it.

We were a little late when we left the house and the driver's license application process took longer than we had expected. Before we knew it we were very late for our own wedding. The fur and the accusations of whose fault it was began to fly. We both wanted to call it off right then and there, but we knew how many people were waiting for us and it would have been too embarrassing. We would have to leave all of our friends waiting at the altar and some of them would have driven over two hours. We grudgingly decided to go through with it.

The service took about five minutes. After a three-minute receiving line we took off for our Chesapeake City reception. It was an achingly gorgeous day. There was a beautiful view of the water from the indoor-outdoor carpeted luncheon room. The food was delicious, especially for the people lucky enough to be able to eat shellfish. I had been allergic to shellfish since age twenty-five when I ate mussels quickly followed by shrimp scampi and then couldn't breathe. I hadn't tried any since.

After we ate and took the requisite wedding photos by the water and in the town's gazebo, we went, with John's friend Tom and his fiancée Joan in tow, to the place we had chosen for the honeymoon. After more photos of the newlyweds among the horses from the adjacent horse farm, Tom and Joan left, leaving us to our first night of wedded bliss.

In our rush to find the perfect honeymoon spot, we had overlooked a lot. When we arrived after the wedding we noticed that not only was the bed and breakfast bordering a horse farm, it was also adjacent to a subdivision. What had seemed like a beautiful colonial home on many acres was on closer inspection a downright dowdy unkempt house with chipping paint that had seen better days. The owners seemed not quite right either, more suited to a trailer park than what we had thought was a manse.

And then there was our honeymoon suite. Dusty red curtains. A host of bisque dolls in Victorian dress with their eyes wide open. When we turned off the lights, there they all were, watching us. We didn't sleep at all, not for the usual honeymoon reasons, but because we thought we were in the middle of some Chuckie-like movie, *The Revenge of the Madame Alexander Dolls.* When the lights were out all we could see were the dolls' eyes. We couldn't shake their stares. And so we spent the night laughing and scaring each other. "Didn't she just move?" John asked.

"Wasn't she over there before?"

"Did you hear what I just heard?"

"Two of them are missing. Where are they?"

"Do you think they'll get us?"

"Are you scared?"

"Are you?"

We got up early, dressed, declined the morning meal included in the rate, drove up the road to our favorite breakfast place, Denny's, and drowned our fears in Grand Slams.

I was so proud that I had planned a wedding, reception and honeymoon in under an hour. Except for the honeymoon it had turned out fine. I thought that had my mother been alive she would have been disappointed that the wedding hadn't been months in the planning and more elaborate. But that is what she always wanted for me, not what I wanted for myself. I was happy with the slapdash wedding I had organized in a flash. Somehow a twice-before-married guy and his forty-nine-year-old bride didn't need the caterer, the flowers, the professional photographer and the five-thousand-dollar gown. That was for kids in their twenties, not for us. I think that my mother would have been impressed with my dispatch in putting the wedding together and with what a lovely day it had turned out to be. We were sorry that neither John's parents nor mine were there, but it is a rare forty-nine and fifty-eight-year-old whose parents live long enough to give them away.

MAKE THAT BURGER WELL DONE

The day after we came home from our horror movie honeymoon we made settlement on our fixer-upper house. Next on our agenda was a visit to John's Philadelphia nephrologist. While sitting around the Warwick pool in Atlantic City the summer before John moved to the United States, we spoke to a woman who also had kidney disease and swore by her doctor, Robert Grossman. He was also listed as one of the best nephrologists in Philadelphia according to ratings by other physicians that appeared for public consumption in *Philadelphia Magazine*. Dr. Grossman spent over an hour with John on that first visit. John told the doctor immediately, as he told every physician he saw, that I was a medical malpractice lawyer, thinking that it made doctors more careful. I thought that it made them more cautious, not necessarily in a good way, and certainly suspicious of me. I couldn't stop John from saying what he wanted to Dr. Grossman. I could only cringe.

By the time he saw Dr. Grossman John had been on the "No Protein Diet" for over a year. John's creatinine was getting higher and higher, signaling progression of the kidney disease, in spite of the diet. Now Dr. Grossman told us John was also malnourished and anemic. He said that while others in his practice believed that a low-protein diet retarded kidney failure, he was not convinced. Dr. Grossman suggested that John go on a more normal diet and begin to get weekly injections to treat anemia.

The doctor also broached the idea of a spousal transplant. Here I was married less than a week and I was already a spouse for transplant purposes. I was dead set against the idea of giving up one of my kidneys, but didn't tell the good doctor or John. No way I was giving up a kidney. I might have appeared on the surface to be altruistic, but not that altruistic. I was angry that the doctor had brought up such an idea in our first meeting. He didn't know us. To be fair he didn't know we had been married only a week. We were strangers to him. I thought he and his suggestion were audacious. And I wasn't about to change my mind, no matter what happened. Not even, as Dr. Grossman suggested, when John became more ill.

When we left Dr. Grossman's office, John didn't have anemia or transplant on his mind. All he was thinking about was where he could get some real food after years of protein deprivation.

We wound up at a French bistro only a few blocks from the doctor's office. John didn't hesitate for a minute. Soon he could make real a fantasy he had had for years. "I'll have a burger."

"How would you like that burger cooked?" asked the waiter.

"Well done."

"Well done?" I asked. It had been so long since he had eaten protein, John had forgotten how to order meat.

"Are you sure you want it well done?" questioned the waiter.

"Make it medium," John said.

He savored that burger when it came and finished it off like a man who had been marooned for years on a meat-free island. He topped off his first real meal in a year with cheesecake. He probably ate more protein that afternoon than he had eaten in the six months before. It was the first time in a long time that I saw him enjoy a meal. Dr. Grossman had given John back his first love, food.

BLENDING THE CAT FAMILIES

When John moved to Philadelphia permanently there were none of the usual family blending problems, since I had no children and Jesse was on his way to London. But there were the cats. We each had two. Mine were Mickey and Sally. John's were Cinder and Ella or, as John's East Indian veterinarian called them, Ella and Cinder because she had no familiarity with the Western children's story after which they were named. My cats were orange, John's black. All were domestic shorthairs, his Canadian and mine American. No fancy pedigrees for us.

We got advice from all corners about how to introduce the two orange cats to the two black ones. First we decided to try the trick that made Mickey and Sally bond. Let's call it "the butter method." I had Sally for over a year when I brought two-month-old Mickey home. I was told to slather butter on

Mickey. If all went as planned Sally would lick off the butter, think Mickey was somehow her baby, and they would be fast friends forever. The butter method seemed to work well for Mickey and Sally. Maybe too well. Soon after Mickey arrived I was awakened in the middle of the night by a loud slurping sound. I looked down to see Mickey with his face buried in Sally's midsection. The butter method had worked so well that Mickey was nursing; it had changed two relative strangers into mother and son.

I saw no reason that the butter method wouldn't work with the cats we now wanted to blend. We figured we would spread butter on all four cats to see what would happen. None of the cats seemed to like the butter massage this time and the only sounds we heard when we finished were loud, menacing hisses. Cinder and Ella took to hiding inside the box spring under our bed. They rarely came out except to eat or to go to the litter box. Mickey and Sally guarded the top of the bed against the interlopers.

Having failed with the butter method we moved on to the only method that worked perfectly—the keeping-them-completely-separated method.

Finally we decided to let them roam freely. Mickey and Sally avoided Cinder and Ella. The new cats were too much for Sally, the oldest of the four. She was also having trouble with the cartons accumulating in my living room in preparation for our move to the new house. One day I arrived home with the groceries to find John sitting outside on the steps. "I think Sally is dead." I went in to investigate. There Sally was in the sunny spot she loved by the window. Rigor mortis had set in. I gathered her up in my arms, kissed her and wrapped her in a towel. We walked her over to the vet's office to be cremated, tears streaming down our faces. I had lost my loyal friend of sixteen years. We expected Mickey to have a difficult transition with all of the milk and companionship Sally had brought to him over the years. He went on as if nothing had happened. He was too busy swaggering around the house, hissing and protecting his turf from the two interloping females.

First-year Blues

John had the jump on me. He had been through two other first years of marriage. This was my first. Even though we had lived together for months in the summers, this was different. It seemed to me so permanent, so irrevocable, although the lawyer part of me knew it was far from irreversible.

To aggravate the fact that every little thing each of us did infuriated the other, we had a home renovation on our hands, an experience that could send even the most stable of relationships out the window. Luckily we could still live in my house while the work was being done. If not for that I think we literally would have killed each other.

I had full responsibility for the renovations. John kept saying, "I wanted a house we didn't have to do anything to."

"There wasn't a house like that," I said again and again in response.

There I was at not quite fifty with a husband who was tired all the time, slept a great deal and left all of the responsibilities to me. I thought that my life had been better when I was alone. I loved him. I hated him. I was schizophrenic.

I was stymied by the renovation. I couldn't understand why, since I grew up in a house where every few years there was a major home improvement project. First my parents knocked a hole in the wall between our kitchen and dining room. Then our neighbors, one by one, did too. I think that all of them copied the design from *Ozzie and Harriet*. We never kept furniture for more than three or four years. One of the rare times during my childhood I ever heard my father raise his voice to my mother was in the house I where grew up on Dorcas Street, just after she refurbished the living room for the fourth time. It was a warm day and my father stuck to the plastic covering on my mother's brand new white raw-silk sofa. "I didn't pay all this money for a sofa to get stuck on the plastic." The plastic disappeared the next day.

As a lawyer I had been making decisions, sometimes on life and death matters, every day. How could I have been paralyzed by deciding what the kitchen configuration should be or what brand of refrigerator to buy? I decided to get professional help, not of the psychiatric kind, although I probably could have used that too, but of the interior design variety. An architect friend looked at the space, said that there was only one arrangement that would work and gave us the name of a reliable kitchen designer. After that everything fell into place. The house was painted, the floors were sanded and refinished, the old kitchen was ripped out and the new one installed, all in six weeks. Compared with kitchen renovation horror stories I had heard, that was breakneck speed.

We moved into our new home in October and things started to calm down. We were getting used to having each other around all of the time. We even started to like it. By the time we reached our six-month anniversary, everything was much better. We were in love again. But John was still exhausted much of the time. His kidneys were getting progressively worse. He was getting paler, in spite of the shots he got each week for anemia.

CHRISTMAS IN MARTINIQUE

John lucked out when he moved to Philadelphia. Not only did he land a job teaching film at the University of Pennsylvania, but by the second year he had both the teaching job and a perk. He was to take twenty-nine students to the Cannes Film Festival.

In December of 1998 we left for Martinique, an island in the Caribbean that is actually a part of France, ostensibly to practice our French to prepare us for John's plum gig the following May.

Martinique was beautiful but very different from the other tropical spots John and I had visited. It was decidedly French. Few people spoke English. Many people had come from France to escape rainy, cold Paris. The tourist culture, particularly the way families related to each other, was like nothing we had seen before. Generations of families came to vacation together, seemingly in harmony. There were pudgy infants in tiny flowered print bonnets, fit and beautifully coiffed mothers, suave fathers, chic grandmothers and grandfathers, even a family dog or two. All had schlepped from Paris to enjoy their holidays. And enjoy them they did. They built sand castles, played catch and soccer, body-surfed, and ate meals at long tables in the hotel dining room. I thought of earlier vacations in Barbados, St. Thomas or Florida, where I had seen American parents plotting ways to escape their children during the day so they could get their St. Tropez tans, while their kids frolicked with other abandoned children at the resort's day camp. Not so the French. All the generations stayed together and frolicked with each other.

I had planned an eclectic vacation, spread over two weeks among three resorts to get a real taste for the country. I hadn't counted on the extent of John's fatigue. Even though I understood why he was so tired I felt frustrated that he slept a lot of the time and wasn't as keen on exploring this new place as I was. Often I wondered if the difference in our energy level was because of our age difference, but the thirty-year-old French women with their sixty-year-old husbands didn't seem to be having the same problems.

We began our Martinique stay at the Meridien Hotel, a sister hotel to the Montreal hostelry where I first spied John, and just a short ferry ride from the capital city of Fort de France. This was the one place where John pushed himself and got quite a bit of exercise. The hotel was perched on a beach that allowed topless sunbathing. John would go off three or four times a day to walk down the beach and stare. While at the Meridien I had a strange experience given that I spoke no better than thirty-year-old high school French. I was getting sandwiches at a local restaurant when a young man who spoke no French at all came in. He was a production assistant on a James Bond movie being filmed on the island. I managed to translate for him so he could get sandwiches and soft drinks for the cast and crew. I flattered myself into thinking that I single-handedly had prevented Pierce Brosnan, one of the Bonds who had succeeded Roger Moore, from starving on some remote Martinique beach.

The second and most eventful part of the trip was spent at Plantation Leyritz, a hotel that was formerly a plantation in the northwest part of the country. We traveled there in our rental car, a petite blue vehicle that looked like a shrunken VW bug. We explored the northern part of Martinique while we stayed at Leyritz. One day we decided to take what the guidebook said was a lovely walk to a picturesque waterfall. We arrived at the ticket booth. There was a warning—people with heart conditions should not attempt the trek. Neither of us knew of any heart conditions we had. I had been diagnosed with a benign heart murmur years earlier, but I didn't think that counted. One of us did have end-stage renal disease, but the warning sign didn't mention that. We forged ahead.

The walk began with a several-mile downhill excursion to a large natural pool. This first part of the walk was a piece of cake. We didn't think then, as you ordinarily don't when going downhill, that we would have a steep uphill climb to get back. We met our guide at the bottom of the hill, a strapping guy who looked like a Dallas Cowboys linebacker, had a broad smile and spoke no English. We put all of our belongings into a plastic container, and although we didn't know it then, we put our lives in his hands. What we encountered next was a maze of rocks and rushing rapids. The guide carried us, sometimes both at once, over the rocks and the swirling water. Now and then he would let us walk on our own but inevitably he would have to save us from ourselves and lift us out of the deep. We finally arrived at the spectacular waterfall, exhausted and happy. He took our photos there, a lucky thing because otherwise no one would have believed that we had made this incredibly dangerous expedition.

Suddenly we were no longer elated. We realized that we would have to go back. Our hero again carried us over the racing water and the perilous rocks, and like some benevolent giant planted us gently on the path back to the entrance. This time it was uphill all the way. We made the climb back, without Superman's help, and finally arrived hyperventilating and exhausted. I felt as if I had used one of my available lives and, by the looks of John, he had used a few of his. His face was literally white. I felt guilty that I had put John's already precarious health through all of this stress. I vowed to myself that from then on I had to be more cautious. We were both grateful that we were still alive. The lawyer in me wondered how many people had died on the trek back and why the warnings weren't better. I found out about the French style of warning later.

We reluctantly moved on to our last stop in Martinique, a Best Western on the east side of the island. The hotel was built to look like a ship, both inside and out. Its most stunning feature was a several-story swimming pool with a particularly precarious drop-off from one level to another. The French tourists seemed not to mind and encouraged their children to swim so that they would be washed screaming over the edge.

The first morning of our stay we sat at a table next to a young couple who were speaking French. John began chatting in English with the young woman seated next to him. He broke the ice by talking about her t-shirt, emblazoned with the name of his graduate school alma mater, Harvard. Turned out that the couple was Parisian, Isabelle and Didier Alfandary. Didier bore a striking resemblance to photos of my father just at the age he met my mother. Isabelle was not just some tourist wearing the Harvard shirt on a whim. She had just completed a fellowship on the twentieth-century American poet E. E. Cummings at Harvard's English Department. The fellowship was the icing on the cake of an already illustrious academic career for the not-yet thirty-year-old. She had a law degree and a Ph.D. in English literature from the Sorbonne. Her English was flawless.

Didier was no slouch either. He was a pulmonologist, who loved to read philosophy. Isabelle's father, too, was a pulmonologist, a famous professor of pulmonology in Strasbourg where Isabelle had grown up. Mutual friends had fixed up Isabelle and Didier with obviously great results. Isabelle told us that her father had always been an Anglophile and people think he looks just like Woody Allen, the director of John's favorite movie, *Annie Hall.*

When the four of us were sitting by the pool later that day I commented to Isabelle about how dangerous I thought the pool was and about the lack of warnings on our harrowing trip to the waterfall. She smiled and said, "The French don't sue over things like that." Apparently the French believe that it is the individual's responsibility to take care of himself and to decide whether something is dangerous or not. All of this no doubt left over from the *liberté* of the French Revolution. That's why there are dangerous swimming pools, teensy weensy cars and no decent warning signs at death-defying waterfalls.

Later that day there was what appeared to be water raining down from the awnings surrounding the pool. Didier suggested that we move because what was pouring down and what eventually spilled on some of the tourists, who weren't as quick-footed as we were, was an acid-based cleaning solution. *Vive La France!*

We spent several days with our new friends discussing literature, politics and our lives. We didn't notice the at-least twenty-year age difference between us.

Christmas was coming, not a big deal for John and me. A Christmas celebration was planned at the hotel. John and I decided that we wanted to go and asked Isabelle and Didier. They said that Christmas wasn't a big deal to them because they were Jewish. We hadn't realized that we had yet another thing in common.

We sadly bid our Parisian friends goodbye a few days after Christmas. They left for France. We left for Philadelphia. We talked about getting together, but those plans made at the end of a vacation often don't pan out. We weren't sure we would ever see each other again. We left Martinique with our French as brushed up as it could be, eager for our sojourn in Cannes.

Are we a match?

When we returned from Martinique, John went to see Dr. Grossman. When his blood tests came back John's creatinine was on the rise—up to 3.9. Normal is about 1.0. John's kidneys were continuing to fail. The other shoe he had been focused on for years was about to drop. Dr. Grossman referred John to the Transplant Clinic for an evaluation. Although John would likely be on the transplant list within a few weeks, it was unlikely that he would get a cadaver kidney, a kidney from a dead person who had signed a donor card or whose family had made the decision for him or her, before John needed dialysis. Dialysis is the process John had always been terrified of, where the patient is hooked up to a machine for four or five hours, three days per week, so that wastes usually filtered by the kidneys are removed from the blood. John was also frightened by the prospect of a kidney transplant. In January 1999 we walked into the Transplant Clinic, located in the basement of what looked like a spanking new facility, the Rhoads Building, at the Hospital of the University of Pennsylvania. The floors were gray marble. The walls maroon. The overall effect, cold and sterile. The Clinic was teeming with people.

This day many were vying for a spot on the transplant list with their families in tow. Others were people who had already had transplants. After a short wait, all of the candidates for the transplant waiting list and their next of kin were herded into a cramped room. At the front of the room was Maral, a registered nurse who was one of the transplant coordinators. She talked about the process of getting a spot on the list, which involved blood testing, medical examinations and psychological testing to insure that a candidate had no diseases that would contraindicate transplant, such as cancer or AIDS, that no heart disease was present that would prevent surgery, and that the patient would be compliant with instructions to take the pills necessary for immunosuppression. Maral, a warm person with a soothing voice, told us all about the transplant list, how the list works, the requirements to get on the list and the recipient's operation. And then she began to talk about a new operation, one the hospital surgeons had just begun to perform, a new operation for donors. "Uh oh. Here we go again," I thought.

Instead of the 8- to 10-inch incision made below the ribs from the front to the back that once was necessary for the donor, Maral explained, now the operation could be done laparoscopically. It involved several tiny puncture wounds and a small incision. I had been adamant for years, whenever John mentioned my being a donor, that I had no plan to give him a kidney. I had been a malpractice lawyer, had seen the results of many botched surgeries and had no intention of putting myself under the knife, any knife, for any reason. I considered any kind of elective surgery, especially plastic surgery, to be pure folly. I intended to wear my laugh lines and all of the others proudly. Better that than to suffer a major infection, stroke or heart attack. No, donating a kidney was out of the question.

My mother always said that I was too much of a "giver," that I was too nice for my own good and people would take advantage of me like they took advantage of my father. It was true that I showered my friends with love and presents, but even I had to draw the line somewhere. And I was drawing the line at my kidney.

Something happened when I really started to listen to Maral. She said that results were better with kidneys from living donors rather than cadavers. The operation could be performed when it was really necessary rather than waiting until a kidney became available. Dialysis could be avoided all together.

I decided to at least have a blood test to see if John and I were compatible. I figured that it wouldn't be much of a problem because it was unlikely that we would be a match. I was quite clear with John that the hospital's taking six vials of my blood was no indication that I would go through with the operation even if we were compatible. Part of me hoped that we would not be a match so that I would appear to be an altruistic heroine and not have to go through an operation. Unfortunately, there were no other candidates for living related donors for John except me. Jesse would not even be considered, Maral said, because there is no guarantee that children of people with kidney disease wouldn't develop the disease later in life. John is an only child, so there were no siblings to volunteer. There was only me and I was at best ambivalent.

A month after our first visit to the Transplant Clinic, John and I came back again so he could have a round of heart tests to clear him for the operation. He was cleared. He was placed on the transplant list. The news was good. His blood type, AB, was one where the list was shortest. He might have only about an eighteen-month wait. If he were lucky, he would get a kidney before he had to go on dialysis. I felt like I might be off the hook.

In March, I sheepishly called Maral as I had been instructed, with my fingers crossed, all the time hoping that I would not be a match. "You are a match," she said happily.

"Thanks," I said, wondering what I would do next.

I figured that I would just let myself be carried along in the process hoping that somewhere along the line I would be ruled out. Not exactly the dedicated wife willing to sacrifice all, even vital organs, for her husband. Not the "giver" my mother always criticized. The cadaver kidney might come along in time. John's kidney function remained stable. I decided to go through to the next level of testing, hoping that some test or another would rule me out. Part of me felt that I was hurtling inevitably toward an operation I didn't want. I wasn't sure I could get off of the roller coaster unscathed.

A PHILADELPHIA LAWYER IN CANNES

We were back in touch with Isabelle and Didier much sooner than we expected. After an exhaustive search eight months before we were scheduled to go to Cannes, I finally landed what I thought was a too-good-to-be-true, reasonably priced apartment right on the Croisette, the fabled main street in Cannes, with a balcony and a water view, just steps from the main film festival venue. This was no mean feat, since most decent hotels and apartments are booked years in advance. Turned out it was too good to be true. The rental agent called in February, just as we were dealing with Maral and matching, to tell us that sadly the owner of our perfect Cannes apartment hadn't renewed his contract with the agency, and the apartment was no longer available. We thought that what had actually happened was that when the owner found out that the agent had rented the apartment for a reasonable price during the Cannes weeks, when he could have gotten ten times as much, he said *"Sacre bleu"* and reneged on the agreement. The agent apologized profusely and offered us a much larger apartment at the same rent but this time much farther from the main festival theater. We knew we couldn't easily dismiss the offer or we would be stuck in the hostel the students stayed in, on bunk beds or worse. Both of us had passed the hostel stage years before. The last professor who took the students to Cannes stayed at a nursing home across the street from the hostel. We weren't ready for the nursing home yet.

I thought Isabelle might be able to help us. I called her and she called the Cannes Tourist Board. One of the people there told her about a young man who coincidentally had just bought and renovated an apartment and was looking for someone to rent it. Isabelle talked to the man and was told that the apartment was brand new, was designed to look like a cabin on a ship, and overlooked a garden. He also said that the apartment was just thirty-five steps from the Palais, the main festival venue. We were skeptical about the distance from the festival, since the apartments anywhere near the Palais are snapped up immediately. Still, we weren't in the position to bargain and we told Isabelle we would take it. Isabelle said she had sent her own check to hold the place. We were very grateful for all that she had done for us, since we really didn't know her that well. We were worried about how the apartment would be and where it would be since we didn't know our landlord at all.

On April 20, 1999, at 4:00 p.m., John and I attended the pre-Cannes meeting with twenty-nine eager college kids who would be accompanying us to the South of France. John distributed the syllabus and fielded questions about the course. Then the other questions came in torrents. "What is the hostel like?" "Is there a curfew?" "Can we wear short skirts to walk up the red carpet?" "What kinds of clothes should we bring?" "How much money do we need?" The students were carefree, about to embark on an incredible European adventure.

We arrived home to "CNN Breaking News." Columbine. A school we had never heard of. A Denver suburb. Mayhem. Students and a teacher killed. An armed camp.

While we coached students on how to dress properly to walk up the red carpet in unreal Cannes, two all-too-real disgruntled, bullied—for what would be the last time—teenage boys had hauled an arsenal of weapons they had been secreting for months in their parents' basements and garages to get the ultimate revenge on the jocks and popular kids who had been taunting them for years. The juxtaposition between the excitement and innocence of the college students we had just met and the tragedy of the dead high school kids in Colorado, who would never get a chance to be college students or spend a summer in France, was jarring.

In May we were off to Cannes. I was worried about going abroad because John had been extraordinarily tired in the last weeks of school. He dragged himself to Penn to teach his classes and came home exhausted. Then he went to sleep. His ruddy skin was now a pasty white all the time. I worried that our going to Cannes with John in this condition was as foolhardy as attempting to navigate the Martinique waterfall. My only hope was that the responsibilities at Cannes would be lighter than his teaching load at home and that the excitement of the place would give him a second wind. The reality of John's disease was that his kidney function would continue to deteriorate until his kidneys no longer worked. The only solutions then would be either dialysis or a transplant. We were already working on the transplant option, I more ambivalently than he.

John lived in fear of dialysis. Who wouldn't? The prospect of being hooked up to a machine four or five hours a day, three days a week, is chilling. Because of how dependent you are on a machine. Because without the dialysis, you die. Because with the dialysis come other ailments. Sometimes infections. Sometimes heart disease. Even death. I worried that John's condition would suddenly worsen while we were in France, and that we would have to find a hospital and make the dialysis decision right then and there in a strange country, in a strange hospital and with a doctor who was a stranger and who didn't speak English. I didn't let John know what I was thinking. I had never realized how much I relied on the doctors that we knew and the hospital we had become all too familiar with in the last few years. I did get special health insurance for our trip. I found out the names of all of the hospitals in the south of France that had nephrology departments and dialysis units.

We never told anyone at Penn about John's kidney condition. We worried that since he only had a one-year contract that he wouldn't be hired for the next semester. We decided not to take a chance. We certainly never told the woman who ran the Penn Summer Abroad program. John was the best person for the Cannes job because he had had so much experience with Cannes and other film festivals. He had been one of the curators of documentary and independent film in the early days of the Toronto Film Festival. I just hoped that we would get through the festival in France with no medical emergencies.

We arrived in Cannes at the address we had been given by Isabelle. The apartment building was as promised, just thirty-five steps from the Palais. But there was no landlord to meet us, in spite of the fact that Isabelle had called a few days before to remind him of our arrival. We were panicky. It wasn't as if we could walk to the nearest hotel and get a room. Everything was completely booked. We knew we had to try to get in touch with the man who had rented us the apartment. We didn't have our cell phone yet. We wouldn't pick it up for a few days. Neither of us was familiar with French pay phones. Why hadn't Miss Fugate taught us to use them? After five or ten jet-lagged minutes of trying to use the phone and a few downright refusals to help from harried French people, a kind middle-aged man stopped to help and dialed the landlord's number. Our landlord was not at home. His father answered the phone. I told him in elementary French that we were at the apartment but his son was not. I remember saying again and again and louder and louder *"Où est votre fils?"*("Where is your son?"), hoping that the volume or the repetition would help him to understand me. He assured me, or at least I thought he did, that he would get in touch with his son and our landlord would be there *"tout de suite."* About an hour and much trepidation on our part later, the twenty-something would-be real estate entrepreneur arrived. He was very businesslike but also very charming. He showed us the tiny studio, which had everything we needed and, as a bonus, a balcony that overlooked what he had described to Isabelle as a garden. It wasn't a garden exactly but the playground of the day care center next door.

We explored Cannes for a few days before the festival, watching workers transform an already breathtaking Côte D'Azur city into a movie festival wonderland. They were preparing the stairs of the Lumière Theater where most of the competition films are shown. When John first told me about going to Cannes, I was excited about the movies but doubted I would be moved by the glitz. Was I wrong! The French really know how to do their glitz. The Palais had red-carpeted stairs. Gendarmes lined the red carpet. Huge movie posters adorned the Belle Epoch buildings on the Croisette.

John got a second wind just as the festival began. His rallying was certainly necessary to navigate the dense Cannes bureaucracy. John's dozen or so visits to Cannes in the past were not of much use. The bureaucracy changes yearly to keep festival veterans on their toes.

The students' arrival also buoyed John's spirits and raised his energy level. The exquisite sunshine didn't hurt either. In Cannes, the sun feels like a life-giving force, with the most extraordinary intensity I have felt anywhere. I kept hoping we would dodge the dialysis bullet at least for a few more weeks. I selfishly didn't want to miss this festival, and I didn't want to have to find a new nephrologist in Cannes.

The festival began and all went well. John had to take long naps to fortify himself. I guessed this would be our last year at Cannes unless John was able to have dialysis there. We knew that there were many dialysis facilities since in the winter, Cannes was the Boca Raton of France, a haven for elderly Parisian snowbirds.

Cannes went off almost without a hitch. We and the students saw hundreds of movies. There was even one instance when my legal training came in handy. Two of the students had broken a glass door when they were sneaking back into the hostel at 4:00 a.m. It turned out that they really didn't need to break in; although there had been a curfew the year before, there no longer was one. Anyway, the glass door was broken, and the hostel wanted to be paid. When the hostel hadn't gotten their money and one of the two glass-breaking culprits was preparing to leave without paying, we received a hysterical phone call from one of the accused students. The hostel didn't want to let the young woman go until she had paid up and they were going to call the police.

I realized that if the threat was real and the gendarmes actually had been called, there was little a Philadelphia lawyer could do. I knew if worse came to worse I could call Isabelle for advice, but I decided to try to handle the mess myself. I told the young woman to pay up in spite of the reasons she had not to. I also asked to talk to the woman who ran the hostel. She of course spoke no English, or if she did, she didn't let me know that. In the best and most assertive French I could muster I shouted, *"N'appelez pas les gendarmes,"* loosely translated, "Don't call the cops." The student paid. The cops were never called. I didn't have to find out what it would be like to practice as a criminal defense lawyer in France without a license. There was always Isabelle but she was in Paris and had never really practiced law. She had just studied it. My greatest fear was that the woman who ran the hostel had a cousin who was the Cannes Chief of Police and once the student got into his clutches it would take many francs and some fancy French legal footwork to get her out of his jail.

It all ended well. We heaved a sigh of relief and went to see the Palme d'Or ceremony, where they give away the top Cannes prizes. We saw the ceremony, not in the Lumière Theater where the celebrities were, but on closed-circuit television in the lobby of the Palais. We then moved on to our real vacation, sans students, films and crowds.

PreGnanT in THE SOUTH OF France

We chose quite by accident an idyllic spot overlooking Gordes, a beautiful sand-colored village in Provence. We only found this house because our rental agent, feeling guilty about pulling the oceanfront Cannes apartment out from under us at the last minute, told us about the Gordes property. He said everyone who rented it loved it and returned year after year. Isabelle expressed some skepticism about our going to Provence, which ever since Peter Mayle's ubiquitous books had become for Parisians a place overrun by American and British tourists, without any genuine French flavor. I was stubborn though, having read the Mayle books. I was aching to taste the bread from the bakery he touted in Menerbes. We were lucky because we would be in Provence in May, not in the summer, when the lavender blooms and the tourists grow like kudzu.

We started our journey to Provence with some small steps, to the Europcar agency in Cannes. We had booked a standard shift even though I could only drive an automatic. The cost of an automatic rental car was prohibitive and I thought we might be upgraded. When we arrived at the agency, the agent was happy to give us a vehicle with an automatic transmission. There were lots of automatic cars left over because of all of the Americans who had rented them for the festival. The agent asked if we wanted a van. That seemed like a great idea since we had certainly over-packed, had bought too many souvenirs in Cannes and were salivating at the prospect of all we could buy at the Provence country markets. Little did we know that our van was far too wide to safely navigate most of the country roads near Gordes.

John drove. We took the very long route so we could look at the Mediterranean as long as possible. What would have been a three-hour direct route took a meandering seven hours. By the time we arrived near Gordes John was enervated and we were both cranky. The view of the gorgeous beige city rising six stories, aiming for the sky, revived us. We easily found Rue des Dilais where we were told we could find our new landlords, the Norths. After a harrowing ride in our too-wide van down a too-narrow path, we saw our little rental in the woods. Our tiny house had an outdoor table and chairs next to an olive tree. We ventured to the swimming pool that overlooked the storybook town of Gordes. The rental agent had more than made up for the Cannes snafu with this little piece of paradise in Provence.

We spent our days prowling through markets in Rousillon, Isle sur la Sorgue, Fontaine de Vaucluse and Carpentras. The markets were varied; each had the most delectable fruits and vegetables. There were apricots with juice that dripped down your chin when you ate them, white flesh peaches, luscious figs, tens of varieties of cherries, myriad cheeses including runny Brie, Port Salut and Camembert. Our usual game plan was to go to a different market each morning, eat a hearty lunch, and later, next to the olive tree in our backyard, enjoy a dinner made up of whatever specialties we could forage from the morning market. John's favorite food in Provence was way off the "No Protein Diet"— sausage loaded with pistachios. We had a wonderful time at our hideaway in Provence. I wondered if we would ever be able to have a normal vacation again if John was on dialysis.

We had hoped that both Isabelle and Didier could meet us in either Cannes or Gordes. Didier was too swamped at work to take off, but Isabelle was able to take the train to Cavaillon, a town not far from Gordes and the undisputed cantaloupe capital of France. We happened into a Cavaillon supermarket just before we picked up Isabelle and were met by a mammoth parquet wood sculpture of a melon. This town was serious about its favorite fruit.

Before Isabelle got off the train, I told John I had a premonition that she was pregnant. Certainly the prophet has a long and prestigious history in the Jewish tradition. John thought I was crazy. He was probably thinking back to our first date in New York when after I predicted it, the guy in the propeller beanie appeared. It hadn't happened since then. Before I get any offers to join Psychics Anonymous I did have some evidence for my theory. I had spoken to Isabelle on the phone a few days before and she complained about being very tired. I could have racked it up to its being the end of a grueling semester of teaching and research for her, but after all she was barely thirty. I never remember being tired when I was thirty.

I don't think that Isabelle was off the train for five minutes when she told us the news. "I'm having a baby in December." Apparently her pregnancy was confirmed in March, just about the time that I was getting the news that John and I were a match for transplant purposes. We were all very excited. I told her of my premonition. We celebrated her pregnancy and my ESP with a Cavaillon all-melon lunch. The melon appetizer, proscuitto wrapped melon, wasn't strange, nor was the melon dessert, melon sorbet with melon and melon candy. It was all a bit much combined with the melon main course. For John, it was melon with cow's cheeks or cow's cheeks with melon, another thumbing of his nose at even a low-protein diet. By the time dessert arrived we were all laughing heartily at all of the prix fixe melon we had consumed in Cavaillon.

We then took Isabelle on a tour of Provence. We went to Menerbes to try to find the bread Peter Mayle wrote about. I'm sure Isabelle thought that a sojourn for great bread was a joke, since all that she had to do to find a near-perfect loaf was to walk around the corner from her Paris flat. Isabelle stayed in Gordes with us for a few days. We dropped her off at the train in Cavaillon, no melon restaurant for us this time, and figured that the next time we saw her we would see Didier and the new baby too, maybe the next year in Cavaillon.

Now and then while we were in France I worried about what Maral had told me, that John and I were a match and what it would mean. I confided in Isabelle about my concern. She said she knew I would make the right decision. I wasn't so sure. John never pressed me about it. When we arrived in Philadelphia, my worry became all-consuming.

JUST GO FOR IT

When we got home from France I felt I was back on the slippery slope to kidney donation. The next step to decide whether I could give a kidney to John was to assess my own kidney function with a 24-hour urine test. All my urine had to be collected over a full day. I remember when John did those tests in Canada. He usually stayed home for the day and worried about what the results would be. I persuaded him to go out and take the bottle with him. I decided to do the same. What I didn't realize was that it was a lot harder for a woman to pee into a bottle than for a man. I kept dribbling over the side. I spent a very unhappy half hour in the ladies room of the Mann Music Center, where the Philadelphia Orchestra plays its outdoor concerts, missing the orchestra, completely missing the specimen bottle and barely missing my skirt.

The next day I arrived at the Transplant Clinic, thinking myself a total failure. Although I had eight years of education past high school, I couldn't manage to provide a proper 24-hour urine specimen. Maral came to the rescue and gave me a plastic boat-like container to pee in, which made collecting my urine much easier. This time I didn't miss. "You can bring the specimen in later in the week," Maral said.

In spite of my urine sample failure I kept my appointment with the nephrologist. I saw Dr. Roy Bloom, a kind-faced, mild-mannered South African man in his forties. I would have rather seen Dr. Grossman, whom I had known for two years but I understood why that was not appropriate. I had to see someone who wasn't interested in John's care so I could get an unbiased opinion about my donor candidacy. Dr. Bloom examined me and asked a lot of questions about my medical history. There was diabetes on my father's side of the family. That might mean I could become diabetic, Dr. Bloom told me. I had in fact had a diabetic episode in my early twenties that was attributed to birth control pills. Dr. Bloom ordered a glucose tolerance test. Although nothing about my age or my recent medical history really warranted it, I thought I should have an echocardiogram and a stress test.

Before I began my judicial clerkship twenty-six years earlier a less than diplomatic physician on the Philadelphia payroll told me, "Your heart sounds terrible." I ran off to a cardiologist who suggested an echocardiogram. The result of the echocardiogram was that I had a benign heart murmur, caused by a mitral valve prolapse. I had taken antibiotics after that diagnosis whenever I went to the dentist. I had also been told to take a stress test every five years. That along with my yearly physical had gone by the boards when my family doctor retired to Hawaii in 1993. I was what could only be described as laissez-faire when it came to my health. That had become one of my defenses to hypochondria. Except for what I had been told was a minor heart defect I just assumed that I would live forever and in perfect health. I had had an echocardiogram the year before I found out John and I were a match. The echo was reported as normal, which really didn't make much sense to me because I thought I had a mitral valve prolapse. Dr. Bloom ordered a renal scan, an echocardiogram and a stress test.

In July I had the renal scan. This was the test to determine if I could have the laparoscopic procedure and to figure out if my kidneys were in good working order. I lay on a table. X-rays of the kidney and bladder were taken. I was given a diuretic so my bladder could fill almost to bursting. I had a near-accident on the diagnostic table but made it to the toilet in the nick of time. Would this be my life from now on—urinating into bottles and near-miss accidents on examining tables? Where was that cadaver kidney compatible with type AB blood anyway? If only it would come soon I wouldn't have to go through all of this.

The day of the stress test and the echocardiogram arrived. I was a little nervous but I figured that since I was an immortal fifty-two year old there was nothing to worry about. The main thing I was worrying about was a really good report, one that showed I was healthy enough to donate a kidney. I asked the echo technician if I still had a mitral valve prolapse. She said "no," but there was something else. I pictured coronary by-pass surgery looming in my future. A second test had to be done that involved injecting me with bubbles, in technical medical lingo called a "bubble test." The bubble test apparently was negative. The technician reassured me that what she had found was nothing serious, just something associated with a greater risk of stroke. And I should talk to a cardiologist about it. I didn't, though, have the benign mitral valve problem I had been told about twenty-something years before. But my heart wasn't "normal" as I had been told the year before. Now not only was I facing a meeting with an endocrinologist to talk about diabetes, but I also had to talk to a cardiologist about my heart and my brain. I had started out being in perfect health and now I had to see two specialists to be cleared so I could have an operation I didn't need.

My usual style would have been to worry obsessively about all of my potential medical problems between the time of my testing in July and my doctor visits in September. Instead, I decided to put all of it out of my mind until the doctor visits actually occurred. My friend Billie had been talking with me over the last few years about the evils of negative prediction. Negative prediction had been my neurotic way of facing my future for as long as I could remember. I spent most of my waking hours imagining all of the horrible ways a particular thing could turn out. My imagination has always been fertile and there was no end to the negative outcomes I could predict. Billie had been telling me that she had been practicing not spinning out a plethora of bad outcomes and just concentrating on facing a particular event without predetermining what would happen. "There's no point in spinning out all of these bad outcomes because we can't really predict how things will turn out, and when we make all these dire predictions they are more often than not dead wrong." I guess the theory is that the bad predictions waste time, and psychic energy is better spent figuring out how to make the outcome good. I decided to try Billie's idea. I wouldn't worry about the doctors' appointments and the possibility that they would condemn me to a nursing home or worse. I just didn't think about the scary echo or the results of my glucose tolerance test and what they could mean for my vitality and my mortality. I just (Are you listening, Woody?) put all of it out of my mind.

John continued to get weaker and weaker. In spite of the shot he got weekly to combat anemia, he had very little energy. I took heart that at the end of our sojourn in France that John's color was better, but when his tan faded the pallor returned. He stayed home and slept most of the day and then fell asleep watching television early in the evening. He became more and more dependent. He could do fewer and fewer chores around the house. I started changing the kitty litter and taking out the trash. John didn't have the energy to cook any more, which for some families wouldn't be so serious, but for ours it was catastrophic. Since my mother worked most of the time and my only living grandmother was a terrible cook, I learned little about cooking growing up. When I began working long hours after I finished law school, I was the queen of takeout. Now, although I was ill prepared, meals became my responsibility too. I could scrape dinner together but anything gourmet became a thing of the past. I had been careful to marry a man who had a flair for cooking. Now he didn't have the stamina to stand at the stove. It was difficult to see John with so little energy. He was losing his spark. His jokes were fewer. He had trouble getting up in the morning. I thought it might just be summer doldrums but it continued into the school year. Sometimes I felt more like a nurse and a maid than a wife.

September came. School started for John, and my first frightening doctor's appointment arrived. I was to see a highly recommended endocrinologist whose name and institution shall remain nameless for reasons that will become obvious. I told him my name and gave him my test results. His cell phone rang. He apologized for taking the call and proceeded to give someone directions to his shore house. While he was doing that, he read the numbers on the records I gave him. He asked me why I was there, and just as I was about to tell him, his cell phone rang again. This time it apparently was a member of his family. He apologized. I told him that I wanted to give my husband a kidney but was concerned I might be diabetic in the future. The cell phone again. When he got off he apologized again and said, "Go for it." It sounded like a high school coach urging a sprinter to his personal best.

"Excuse me?" was all I could say.

"If it's what you and your husband want, just go for it. Even if you got diabetes tomorrow it would be twenty years before your kidney would go."

I never liked cell phones. I knew I had to see a different endocrinologist.

My experience with the cardiologist was different. I had succeeded for two months in keeping myself from being upset about the prospect of being told I would be a cardiac cripple. Now the day I would get the terrible news had arrived. I had done all I could to get the echo from twenty-five years before. No dice. I did get the videotape of the last year's "normal" echo. I brought the videotape with me, sat in the waiting room and did all the negative predicting I had not done in the months before—surgery, heart attack, stroke, complete bed rest, life no longer as I had known it, being condemned to a nursing home, death. By the time I saw the cardiologist's nurse I was a mess. When she began asking me questions I started to cry. She assured me that Dr. Martin St. John Sutton, the cardiologist I was about to see and the director of Penn's cardiac testing labs, was a lovely man who would tell it to me straight. I was immediately thrown. I had assumed that Dr. St. John Sutton was an African American woman, and that she and her husband had hyphenated their names. I have no idea why I assumed that, but the thought made me feel good. I thought I would be able to relate to her and if she had really bad news to tell me, I could take it. All I hoped now was that the doctor had no imminent plans at his summer home and that he didn't have a cell phone.

Into the room strode a very tall white man with a British accent. The doctor's name wasn't the modern way of blending two families. It wasn't at all modern. One of his ancestors had probably said at one time or another, "Pity we lost India." I didn't see any sign of a cell phone. The doctor saw that I was upset and he was very kind. He was completely focused on me. He was not at all distracted. He kept saying, "You're a good person." I knew that. What I wanted to know was whether I was a "you have two months to live person," a "you could have a stroke at any time person" or a "you need immediate cardiac surgery person." Dr. St. John Sutton told me that I had a quite common heart defect, a small opening in the wall between the two upper chambers of my heart, which occurs when the heart hasn't fully developed in utero. He said that there is an increased risk of stroke in people who have this problem and that the condition is not life threatening. I did need to take an aspirin a day to prevent strokes. I felt much better. He said that nothing about the condition of my heart would prevent me from having the kidney surgery. My relief about dodging the heart surgery bullet was quickly replaced by anxiety about not dodging the kidney donor bullet. The cardiologist also told me I couldn't be so cavalier about my health. It was important that I see a doctor regularly, especially if I had only one kidney and had a family history of heart disease and diabetes. Here was another result of the "bubble test." Pop went the immortality bubble.

In October I summoned all of the little nerve I had left and went to see a second endocrinologist. I hoped against hope that this one had no cell phone. I wasn't sure if it was the earmark of the specialty. I felt good as soon as I entered the waiting room. All of the many people there told me that they loved Dr. Stanley Schwartz. They talked about his always being available, of his being very kind. Dr. Schwartz actually ventured into the no man's land of the waiting room to greet his patients, a lost art among many doctors. He had a warm smile. He was balding, about five foot six inches tall. After a bit of Jewish geography we found that we grew up in the same neighborhood in northeast Philadelphia at the same time. He had gone to Northeast High. I told him that because I could no longer stomach the cruelty of the nasty girls in junior high that I escaped to Girls' High, a forty-five minute bus ride away from the neighborhood. Dr. Schwartz, after looking at my tests, taking a history and talking with me without benefit of cell phone, told me there was only a ten percent chance I would become diabetic as a result of the surgery and that I would likely do fine with only one kidney. That was what I needed to know. Dr. Schwartz said to let him know when the surgery was scheduled and he would see me in the hospital before the operation. When I left he said, "You would have done fine at Northeast."

I felt as though I was being propelled into the decision to give John my kidney. There seemed to be no more excuses, although my mind raced desperately to find some good reason not to subject myself to what was for me totally unnecessary surgery. I could find no good reason or even a bad one to deny John my kidney. He was getting more and more tired. Excruciating leg cramps plagued him. John's jokes, which he would sprinkle liberally in most conversations, stopped. He always said that one of the things he most loved about me was that I always laughed at his jokes no matter how many times I had heard them before. As perimenopause set in beginning in the mid-1990s, I really didn't remember those old jokes, and from that time on I really was laughing at them as if they were brand new. To me they were, since I couldn't remember much of anything. Now John rarely told jokes and I rarely laughed. He looked like a walking ghost. Dr. Grossman was starting to talk to him about dialysis, the possibility that had always been his greatest fear. The doctor wanted to put a shunt in his arm a few weeks before dialysis so that the shunt could ripen before the dialysis began. John was getting more and more panicky. It's very difficult to watch someone you love becoming more ill. It's even more difficult when you know you can do something to help and feel ambivalent about the possibility.

By October we were poised on the edge of a transplant operation, John without options and I without excuses. And we had yet to meet the surgeons who would perform our surgeries. Our surgeries. A family that goes under the knife together encounters strife together? Are forever husband and wife together? Gets sliced together?

Maral set up an appointment for us with Dr. Ali Naji, one of the transplant surgeons. We knew little about Dr. Naji, although all of the employees in the Transplant Clinic and the patients we met in the waiting room touted his virtues as a surgeon and as a person. I was skeptical about Dr. Naji's reputation as a wonderful person. Most of the surgeons I had ever met were full of themselves, narcissistic to beat the band. Surgeons often think that they are gods or at least anointed by God to cure the ills of the world while brandishing knives. I thought that transplant surgeons could only be worse, since what they did should properly be venerated. They really were playing God, giving life where there soon would not be any at all except maybe only the life of being tied to a dialysis machine for fifteen hours a week. I didn't know how anyone could come away from that veneration without a swelled head.

Dr. Naji certainly was different from what I expected. When we first met him, he was impeccably dressed in a black and white tweed blazer and dark slacks, very handsome, with salt-and-pepper hair. From the beginning he was very kind. He was of Iranian descent, which was at first a bone of contention for John since he usually only liked being treated by Jewish doctors. I think the reason had something to do with the fact that he imagined that if a doctor was of the same religious brotherhood he would take more care in the treatment. Having seen many malpractice cases with names like *Goldstein v. Levin* and *Berger v. Greenbaum,* I knew that that wasn't necessarily true. You had just as much chance of a medical mistake being made by someone of your own religion as by someone who wasn't.

Because of my medical malpractice background, I doubted that Dr. Naji's explanation of the surgeries and their outcomes would be legally adequate. Maybe that was an excuse I could use to back out. All might not be lost. Maybe I could find a way out of only the third surgery of my life after a botched tonsillectomy at age six. The tonsillectomy hadn't gone well and resulted in a second surgery in the middle of the night and an office procedure by a doctor who yanked out the dressing in my throat without the benefit of even local anesthesia.

My theory that Dr. Naji's explanations wouldn't pass the informed consent test didn't fly. He meticulously explained how my operation he called "the closed procedure" would be done. He described several small incisions in the midriff area made for the insertion of a camera and other instruments and then a small longitudinal incision below the belly button where a bag would be inserted. The left kidney would be freed from its single ligament. (Apparently God or something else had made it that way in most people, maybe for ease in transplant. The right kidney is attached by two ligaments.) Then the kidney would plop in the bag (my words, not his) and would be pulled out. I learned too that the bag looked like a butterfly net. I liked the romance of that image. But none of this explanation seemed the least bit romantic to me. I didn't want to hear about the risk of infection or the risk of a premature blind date with The Grim Reaper. Dr. Naji said he was pretty sure that the closed procedure could be done on me, but there was a slight chance that the procedure might have to be converted to an open procedure complete with its long incision circling my left side. Dr. Naji said that more than twenty laparoscopic procedures had been performed at Penn since they started doing them in the last year. Only one had to be converted to an open procedure.

John asked, "Is there any difference in how viable the kidney is if the donor procedure is open or closed?" I interpreted this question as terribly narcissistic. In his defense he was literally fighting for his life, his health, his vitality. I knew that for me the difference between the two procedures was that the open procedure meant more cutting, more pain, longer recuperation, a greater risk of infection and a bigger chance that my rendezvous with the Reaper could come much earlier than I had bargained for. In answer to John's question Dr. Naji said that a kidney removed laparoscopically sometimes takes longer to function than one removed in an open surgical procedure, because the kidney relates better to human touch than to the touch of the butterfly net. I felt a little guilty that I didn't ask Dr. Naji to perform the open procedure that involved the huge incision around my torso to insure John a better functioning kidney. I don't think I would have gone through with the procedure at all if I was sure it would be open. If that shows a lack of character, so be it. Just the chance, small as it was, that the procedure might have to be converted from closed to open threw me into a panic.

Dr. Naji said that he would be the surgeon who would transplant my kidney into John. Dr. Markmann would perform my surgery. By the time we had spent one hour with Dr. Naji we were convinced that only he could make sure my surgery was properly performed and only he could properly place my harvested kidney into John. Something about that word "harvest" conjured for me the image of my dysfunctional family around the mahogany table in the house I grew up in gorging ourselves on Thanksgiving turkey and pumpkin pie. I noticed that Dr. Naji had spent more time talking with me than with John. I guess it was because I was the person with the most to lose and the least to gain. I was the healthy, or at least relatively healthy, person some doctor had to operate on. I was the one who was going to make the transplant possible. Without my agreement there would be no lifesaving here or at least no saving from dialysis.

"Will you be the surgeon?" John asked tentatively, having forgotten all of his craving for a Jewish doctor.

"Unless Mary Tyler Moore needs me," Dr. Naji replied.

Wait a minute, I thought. What does Mary Tyler Moore have to do with this? All that she was for me was that woman on TV who lived in Minneapolis, threw her hat in the air and whose boss was Mr. Grant. When I was a teenager, I had difficulty relating to her. Her Jewish friend Rhoda I could relate to. And now Mary could have an impact on my life. She could take Dr. Naji away just when John and I needed him. Seems that there was a good reason that Mary and Dr. Naji might have to be together around the time our surgery was scheduled. Mary was no longer throwing her hat in the air. Now she and Dr. Naji were honorary chairmen of the Juvenile Diabetes Association. They were desperately seeking a cure for that devastating disease. If Mary called there was good reason for Dr. Naji to answer. He often had to accompany her to important meetings like a recent one at the Clinton White House. John and I hoped that the White House didn't call anytime in the next few months. I rationalized that Mary was unlikely to throw her hat in the air asking for Dr. Naji's presence in Washington in December, when the transplant would likely be, because most of Congress would be heading home for the Christmas recess. I worried about fundraising, though, which is usually big before the end of the year. When we walked out of our first consultation with Dr. Naji we joined the rest of the people in the Transplant Clinic on the Naji bandwagon.

Things came to a head a few weeks after we met Dr. Naji when Dr. Grossman told John that elective transplant surgery dates were filling up for December. We wanted to have the surgery in December, if we were going to do it at all, so that John could avoid dialysis, and so that he would be able to go back to teaching in January. We knew that we were being optimistic about his immediate return to school but we thought that five weeks would be enough time for him to recuperate. We were wary of letting the School of Arts and Sciences or the English Department know about the transplant. John taught at the pleasure of the dean and we didn't want him to lose the job he loved because people didn't understand kidney disease and transplant. I knew that Penn could not fire John because of the transplant, but I also knew that he was only hired on a yearly basis and they could refuse to renew his contract. I also didn't want to deal with a lawsuit about all of this if they fired him or didn't rehire him once they learned about the condition of his kidneys or about the transplant surgery.

Summoning up all of the courage I could muster, I called Maral for a surgery appointment. We were hoping for December 10, the day after John's last day of teaching. They didn't operate on Friday. The first appointment after that, and the only appointment available in December, was on December 14. December 14th it was. For me the decision was made, almost in spite of myself. I had come this far. I didn't think that there was any way to back out now. I felt like a little lamb in a stockcar inexorably bound for the slaughter. I learned later that the donor could always back out, just by telling a doctor at the Clinic. The doctor would then determine that the donor was for some reason or another not a good match and never reveal why. I'm sure that they told me this somewhere along the line. I had for some reason not heard them.

I was furious at all of the people who refused to sign donor cards so that their organs could be harvested after they died and donated to people who needed them. Why were all of these people going to their graves with their organs, where the crucially needed kidneys, livers and hearts would turn to dust? If there were enough organs plucked from cadavers, thousands could live and no one like me would have to contemplate unnecessary surgery while they were alive to give someone they loved a vital organ, one the donor might need later in life.

Now I had to start practicing the "no negative prediction" method in earnest. I did that as best I could and concentrated on what would make me feel good during the hospital stay and surgery and how I could prepare the house for our convalescence. "The method" was not working so well for me, since I was living with the king of negative prediction. John was busily predicting the worst outcomes and telling me about them in gruesome detail. "Do you think I will be able to go back to work in January? It's not much time. What if I can't?" "How much do you think it will hurt?" And the clincher, "Are you scared?"

I had to ignore John's ruminations as much as I could and became for the first time in our relationship cold and not empathetic. I had to be that way for my own good. I was precariously on the edge of panic for two months in anticipation of December 14. I had to be careful not to fall over the precipice.

I also kept myself very busy getting the house and my office in order to prepare for our convalescence. The office was easy. Home was more of a challenge. I decided to stock the house so that no one would need to carry anything heavy in or out for two months after the surgery. Now, don't get me wrong. Our house was always well stocked and could have served as a decent air raid shelter as it was. I had learned from my mother that it was some kind of a sin not to have a several months' supply of toilet paper and soup at the ready at all times. I had no idea how long we would be disabled. I just wanted to be prepared. My quest for preparedness also let me keep busy in my favorite pastime—shopping. I have always loved shopping, which is not synonymous with buying. I have always seen shopping as a kind of sport, a woman's answer to watching football. I remember one shopping spree when my mother was terribly ill and had been admitted to the hospital for the fourth or fifth time in two months. I was impossibly stressed and went to a small discount clothing store near the hospital, handled most of the merchandise, tried on some, bought nothing and felt some of the stress melt away. So, before the transplant I went into high acquisition mode.

Tropicana probably sold more than its quota of Grovestand, the lots-of-pulp orange juice, in Philadelphia in November. I filled our oversized refrigerator with twenty cartons of juice, set to expire at the end of January 2000, when I figured I could shop again and lift heavy cartons. I filled the basement with ginger ale, grape juice and cranberry juice. The kitchen cupboards were chock full of hot and cold cereals and salt-free potato chips. The freezer was full to bursting with frozen soup, ravioli and lasagna. You-name-it, it was in the house.

I concentrated on food that was easy to prepare and not perishable. I was stocking up for what would be our version of an eight-week winter storm. I delighted in the shopping and in dragging the heavy bags into the house. It was a sign of my independence, my strength. I worried what it would be like not to be able to lift, drag and empty bags filled to the breaking point. I couldn't imagine not being able to do these mundane jobs that recently had risen in my estimation to exalted tasks. I happily emptied the kitty litter and cheerily bundled up the trash and schlepped it outside, all the while wondering what it would be like even in the short term to not be able to do those things. I realized that I had always taken my stamina for granted, never expecting that anything would interfere with my good health.

In the last weeks before the surgery my negative predictions broke through and I went through a host of "What if this is my last _____?" My last supermarket trip. My last kitty litter change. My last trash haul. The last time I pick up my cat Mickey. The last time I can sort out a complex legal problem. I became terribly worried about my independence, my physical health and my mind.

Sometime in November, Brent, one of the Toronto *minyan* men, went to Winnipeg to donate a kidney to his brother. Brent tried to talk to me before his procedure but all I could do was to wish him and his brother well and hand the phone quickly back to John. I was too close to my surgery and terribly afraid to join the brotherhood/sisterhood of transplant donors. Under normal circumstances I would have called Brent to find out how the operation went and how he was feeling. Not this time, though. I was just barely holding my anxiety about my operation in check. The last thing I needed was to talk to someone who had just had a surgery similar to the one I was to have. In fact Brent was having the open donor procedure. They weren't doing the closed procedure in Winnepeg yet. Brent was having a procedure that for me was the worst-case scenario. I didn't want to find out anything about what my worst possible convalescence would be like. I didn't want to know how long Brent's scar was, or how much pain he suffered. John didn't call Brent after his transplant or before ours. I didn't prod him to do that. I always felt bad about my callousness toward Brent, but it was pure self-preservation.

A special House in the country

A squib in *Variety* caught my eye just about a month before our surgeries. Oscar Hammerstein's house, Highland Farms, in Bucks County was for sale for what seemed like a bargain price, $1.2 million. From the *Variety* blurb it sounded wonderful—five acres, a large manor house and a pear-shaped swimming pool, because pears were Hammerstein's favorite fruit. Maybe this was the country escape we had been looking for intermittently for the past few years. I called the listing agent, Adam Shapiro. He said the price had been dropped to $875,000. Our lucky day. Well, not quite, since our country house budget was more in the neighborhood of $200,000. Anyway, the Hammerstein house wasn't just any house. It had a great provenance. Some of the best Broadway songs had been written right there. I had read every book I could get my hands on about Oscar Hammerstein and Rodgers and Hammerstein. Me, the kid who had spent every weekend in my basement or in the basement of one of my friends or another singing and dancing to the original Broadway cast albums of "South Pacific," "The King and I" and "The Sound of Music." I had always unabashedly loved Hammerstein because he had written all of those wonderful words, even the words I had heard in my mind from "Some Enchanted Evening," when I met John on that corner in Montreal. According to the many biographies I had read about Hammerstein and Stephen Sondheim, "O, What a Beautiful Mornin'" was written right on the porch of the Doylestown house, and Sondheim had learned how to write musicals in the Hammerstein living room. The entrepreneurial part of me dreamed of a school for budding lyricists on the Hammerstein grounds. We made an appointment for that weekend for what could have been the worst impulse buy of our lives.

We arrived in Doylestown early and had lunch. The scuttlebutt at the restaurant was that the Hammerstein house had already been sold. We were crushed. Our live-in-the-moment-just-before-surgery mentality was that we could sell our house in Philadelphia, cash in all of our stock, take a huge mortgage and open a bed and breakfast, something neither of us had contemplated before. I thought that I could get a host of grants, start a foundation and open a refuge for young lyricists, the Puff Daddys or P. Diddys of the future. And now someone had bought that dream out from under us. We figured we would meet Adam Shapiro anyway, as we promised we would. At the very least we would see the place where Hammerstein got his inspiration.

We drove down a long driveway. The house was on our right. And we saw the problem immediately. To the left of the driveway was the highway. The porch, where Hammerstein wrote the famous song from "Oklahoma" that extolled the beauty of a morning in the countryside, no longer faced a cornfield and the many acres of Hammerstein's farm. Now the porch overlooked a busy road with a shopping center across the street. There were four-lane highways on two sides of the property. If Hammerstein were writing on the morning we saw his country place, the corn in the song might have been as high as a tractor-trailer driver's eye. Shapiro told us that the scuttlebutt we heard in Doylestown was wrong—the house was still for sale.

Although I knew immediately that I wouldn't sell my farm to buy Hammerstein's, I still wanted to see the inside of the house. John wasn't as sure as I was that the Hammerstein house wasn't for us. As we walked around the property he kept offering suggestions for killing the highway noise, from thermal pane windows to more trees to a huge fence. But even John had no solution for the diesel and gas fumes wafting from the highways that surrounded Hammerstein's once idyllic hideaway. Seems that the state needed some land to construct highways and expropriated much of the Hammerstein property for its purposes.

As we toured the house we saw the study where Hammerstein wrote his lyrics, standing at an elevated desk, and the living room where Hammerstein told a teenaged Sondheim that the lyrics for the first show he wrote for the nearby George School were terrible, and if Sondheim really wanted to learn how to write a musical, Hammerstein could help him. And help him he did, right there in that Doylestown house. The house had a peacefulness about it, interrupted only intermittently by the drone of sixteen wheelers outside.

We were lucky that the house defied the old real estate maxim of "location, location, location" or we might have made the impulse buy of the century. The Hammerstein house just wouldn't work for us. We had to find another way to deny our imminent surgeries, or face them.

our ASIAN THANKSGIVING
and DOWN TO THE WIRE

We decided to spend Thanksgiving without our families and without anyone else's family. We went to Atlantic City to spend a quiet Thanksgiving near the beach. When Thanksgiving actually came we both craved a traditional meal, and we figured that we could find that at one of the huge casino buffets. We chose the Hilton, which was only a few blocks away from our apartment. It was pouring; the rain was driving toward the ocean as we set out on the long, wet four-block walk to the hotel. We figured that it wouldn't be too crowded. Who goes out to dinner at a casino on Thanksgiving? We arrived at the Hilton to find a block-long line. Several maitre d's asked us if we had reservations.

"Reservations?" we asked.

"It is one of our busiest days."

"We had no idea."

One of the maitre d's took pity on us for our naiveté and ushered us to the lone empty table in a huge ballroom.

We found ourselves in a room that seated about a thousand, two of the very few white faces. Everywhere there were Asians for whom Thanksgiving is apparently no big thing. But gambling is. They were bussed in by the savvy casino operators for a day of gambling capped off by a huge buffet. It was one of the few times that I had eaten out on Thanksgiving when there was no shortage of turkey and cranberry sauce. Everyone else opted for the Shrimp Lo Mein and the Kung Pao Chicken.

On our way home from the Thanksgiving weekend we stopped at a huge Acme supermarket in South Jersey for what I thought would be my last big shop before the operation. I savored every minute in the gigantic, spanking clean store. I stocked up again on orange juice, ginger ale, pretzels and potato chips. The smiling checkout clerk asked, "Are you having a party?"

John, who was ordinarily closed-mouthed about the transplant, said, "No, we're having operations." Then he pointed to me with pride, "She's giving me a kidney."

Then she hugged us, this perfect stranger. "What are your names? My aunt likes to pray for people. I'll tell her to pray for you."

"John and Joan," I said.

We were happy to accept all offered prayers, no matter what the denomination of the person who prayed. As the surgery approached the prayers for our successful recovery were mounting. Our friend Maureen Callahan told us that her mother Mae had sent a contribution to the pink nuns. As you might have guessed, these nuns dress in pink, not the pastel pink you would automatically think of but hot pink. They live in the heart of Philadelphia's bustling Art Museum area but, since they are cloistered, don't venture outside on the block where they live or to the city beyond. Toni, Jack, Maryann and Jim were praying for us by lighting candles in their Catholic churches in New Jersey. Billie was saying a prayer for good health, a *meshaberach,* for us at her synagogue in Germantown. *Meshaberachs* were being said for us in Toronto too.

A few weeks before surgery I talked to my Girls' High chum Jeanne, who had a wildly successful graphic design business in Manhattan. We had been through a lot together. She had been with me at that Girard College social. Jeanne and I had always been supportive of each other but I always felt somewhat competitive with her. She had been the president of Girls' High and a very accomplished artist when we were growing up. In our conversation that December day she told me that she had had laparoscopic surgery a few years before and was back at work two weeks later. I decided that if Jeanne could recover in lightning speed, so could I. Jeanne also told me that she had laid her quick recovery to being in excellent physical shape before the surgery. I wasn't in such great shape, but there were still two weeks to go. I took to walking the two miles back and forth to work every day. I also added walking down the eighteen flights of stairs at my office to my fitness schedule. No way Jeanne was going to recover faster from her operation than I would from mine.

As we got down to the wire in the few days before the surgery my friends kept suggesting that we hire someone to take care of us after the surgery. Dr. Naji said that I could stay on as long as John did in the hospital, for five or six days after the operations. That seemed like more than enough time for me to recuperate fully. Yet more denial. I figured that I could manage, what with the air raid shelter in the basement stocked with toilet paper, ginger ale and tunafish, and the refrigerator stocked with everything else. I thought if worse came to worse, I could impose on my friends for a night or two. My failure to hire someone to help us for a week when we came home from the hospital was one of the most serious errors I made.

School ended for John. All of his papers were graded. He was getting up every night in the middle of the night and cataloguing his anxieties to me. Ms. Denial, as I had affectionately dubbed myself, had the daunting task of ignoring not only my anxieties but his too.

Our friend Bonnie had us over for brunch the day before we were scheduled to go to the hospital, our "Last Brunch," the Jewish version of the Last Supper. She took Polaroids. When I saw the photos, I realized we both looked terrible. I thought that I was doing much better than I looked.

When we arrived home from Bonnie's for what I hoped would be a relaxing evening before going to the hospital the next day, I found the first of several what I interpreted as passive aggressive passes from The Girl with the Hat, who had still refused to go away. This time it was a voicemail wishing us good luck in our operations. I had told John I don't know how many times that I didn't want her contacting me. I assumed that he had passed on the information. It was particularly difficult for me in my fragile pre-transplant state. I was furious; a reaction she would have known would have occurred had her head not been so firmly implanted up her hat. So John and I spent yet another evening embroiled in a debate about why John didn't have the balls to tell The Girl with the Hat to get permanently lost. I thought about telling John to forget about my kidney and to try to get one from her. Maybe her kidney would come with a little beret.

Just before falling asleep the night before we left for the hospital, I lay awake thinking. It went something like this. Marriages don't last forever. Especially John's. I was his third wife and The Girl with the Hat was another significant relationship.

What if John and I split up and he left me for another woman, with my kidney? There would be no way to get it back.

I imagined future scenes. In one we were walking down the street arguing. "I'm leaving," John would say.

"Do what you want, but I want my kidney back."

"You'll never find a surgeon who will do that."

And so there I would be minus both a lover and a kidney, facing old age alone and without a vital organ.

THE DAY BEFORE

The day we leave for the hospital. The day before the surgery. I'm up at dawn. John was up all night. Tempers were frayed over The Girl with the Hat's tossing it in the ring again. We said goodbye to Mickey, Cinder and Ella. Some part of me, not the part that had abandoned negative prediction, thought that it was for the last time. We had to be at the transplant clinic at 9:00 a.m. for blood tests to see if we were still compatible. Based on how we were getting along under the stress of the impending surgery, I was not so sure. John was much more verbal than usual in expressing his gratitude for what I was doing. He also said he wasn't sure that he could do the same for me. Was this yet another reason to back out now? We had the blood tests and then went to our rooms on the fourth floor of the Rhoads Building. The clinic did all of our paperwork so we did not need to tell any more people our birth dates and social security numbers.

We each had a private room. I'm not sure if it was for infection control—less of those controls were necessary for me than for John—or because everyone had separate rooms. I was sad to find out that we wouldn't be in the same room. We had been sleeping in the same bed for the last two and one-half years except for occasional business trips. My room was palatial, if a hospital room can be called palatial. I named it "The Four Seasons Room" since it looked like a luxurious room in an upscale hotel, complete with upholstered love seat and armchair, wood paneling and a marble bathroom. The room had a lovely view of the University of Pennsylvania campus.

John's room was more spartan. No marble. No wood paneling. Not much of a view. We learned later that the donor regularly gets the more luxurious room, a kind of "thank you" from the hospital for making one more transplant possible. As a further thank you to the donor, this time from the recipient's insurance company, the donor pays no hospital or doctor bills for the surgery. They are all paid by the insurance company of the person who gets the organ. Apparently paying for both the donor's and recipient's charges is cost-effective for the insurance company because if all goes well the company avoids paying for years of costly dialysis.

We delivered our living wills, the legal documents that let the hospital know when we give permission to pull the plug in case of catastrophe, to our nurses and insisted that our allergies, his to penicillin and mine to iodine, be emblazoned on the front of our charts. No one was really sure that I was allergic to iodine, but since I was allergic to shellfish, it was a good bet.

My nurse came into the room and ordered me out of my clothes and into an open-air hospital gown. I resisted for a while, insisting that I keep on my street clothes. I had brought several brightly colored flannel nightgowns with me but ultimately suc-

cumbed to the hospital-issue nightie. I was becoming institution-
alized without much of a fight.

So far, nothing seemed too scary. John came to in my room,
the no-brainer choice, while we were poked, prodded and talked
to by a procession of bright young men, the residents and fellows
in nephrology and transplant. My nurse returned and used my
arm again and again for a pincushion, hoping each time that on
this try she could get a vein. After the fourth attempt she struck
pay dirt. I learned later that every nurse should get only one
miss. After the first miss, it is time to ask for a phlebotomist.
They rarely miss their mark. No one had much time to spend
with us. We had inadvertently planned our surgeries for the
busiest time for the transplant service. Because of holiday car
accidents and suicides, a raft of organs were coming up for people who had waited years. All of the beds in the ward were full.
I thought that we had beaten the holiday rush by a week but we
were in the thick of it.

Our blood test results came back. In spite of all of the tension
of the last few months and the recent reemergence of The Girl
with the Hat, we were still a match. The operation was a go.
John's creatinine was 7.8. Mine was 0.8, better than normal.

An anesthesiologist came in to talk with me, a handsome,
tall African American man. He told me all of the things he had
to tell me, all of the things I knew and all of the things I really
did not want to hear. As with any operation there was the risk
of infection, heart attack, stroke and death. I winced. I hoped he
hadn't noticed. I was still in my stoic mode. What was I doing?
Could I bolt? Just as the kindly anesthesiologist was leaving I
caught sight of his nametag. I had missed his name when he
first introduced himself. I was preoccupied with my own
thoughts, the foremost of which was, "What have I gotten
myself into?" He was Dr. King. I felt safe. The namesake of the

Civil Rights Movement was taking care of me. Everything would be all right, I thought. I told Dr. King that he had a wonderful name. I'm sure he thought that I was suffering anesthesia effects before it was even administered.

When I called my office voicemail after talking with Dr. King, I had many messages. I thought that I had cleared most of the problems away before I went to the hospital. I hadn't told my clients about the surgery. I figured within a few days I could return phone calls and make excuses. We had told John's colleagues that we were headed for South Beach in Florida. That would work for me too if it was necessary. As usually happens before a vacation or other work hiatus, all of the people I have ever met call to ask advice about some urgent problem, real or imagined. I managed to answer whatever I could over the phone. When I couldn't solve a problem that I determined wasn't really urgent, I told them I was going out of town and would get back to them after the first of the year. Everyone I talked to seemed satisfied. I could put work behind me at least for a few days.

Next came the hospital food. I took off the cover on my tray and a grotesque smell filled the room. It was the hospital's version of shepherd's pie. John, who rarely met a meal he didn't like, wolfed down the food. I settled on a dinner of graham crackers and skim milk.

We kissed good night and wished each other luck. I took John's hands in mine. I stared at his face for a long time. I worried I might never see him again. His skin was almost grey and those blue eyes I had fallen in love with in Montreal no longer sparkled. We kissed again. John went back to his room. I took my sleeping pills and went to bed.

MY LEFT KIDNEY

5:00 a.m. December 14, 1999. I held in most of my anxiety until I woke up. Then I panicked. Now I had to put my left kidney where my mouth was and undergo major surgery for no good medical reason. Was I nuts? What was I doing? Would I survive? I was a mess. Then they came for me with the litter. I figured that I could still jump off and run away with my hospital gown exposing the most ample part of my anatomy. A kindly young man wheeled me through a maze of hallways to the operating room. I allayed my anxieties and my flight impulse by chatting with him. He had the sunniest disposition. We talked about the blues and about a blues group he loved. He said, "God bless you" as he left. I so wanted to believe in God.

When the orderly left me in the chrome-lined anteroom outside of the operating theater, I began to hope in my heart of atheist hearts that there was a God. I no longer felt like I could escape. I wasn't sure which direction I would go in. I was resigned to my fate, whatever that would be. A calmness came over me. Here I was at the operating room. Whatever was going to happen would happen. It was all in the doctors' hands now. All I could do was to hope for the best. Then Dr. King came by. I felt much better. I decided he was my guardian angel. Whenever he was around, I thought, I would be fine. He would take care of me.

While I was assiduously attempting to keep myself calm in the months before the operation, I figured out what would make me feel better and what I could do to promote that good feeling. My enthusiastic food shopping was one approach. Another thing I decided that I wanted to do was to ask the anesthesiologist and the surgeon to talk to me during the operation even though I wouldn't be conscious. I don't know why I thought that would make me feel better. I just thought I might get something subliminally that would help. I had been too ashamed to ask Dr. King about it when I first met him, but now that I thought that he was my guardian angel, I decided that my asking and his agreeing were not outside the realm of possibility. I asked. He agreed, saying, "I believe in positive reinforcement." I felt much better. I later realized that asking for that connection even when I was asleep made me more to him than just an anesthetized lump, more like a real person he was rooting for.

Dr. James Markmann, my surgeon, stopped by before the surgery. It was the first time I had met him. Dr. Naji had given me the option of meeting Dr. Markmann well before the surgery. It probably would have been a good idea. I had declined. I was doctored out.

When they wheeled me into the operating room, Dr. King was there and I met Dr. Rebecca Barnett, the other anesthesiologist, a diminutive white woman. It was sometime during my banter with Dr. Barnett about her growing up in Zimbabwe that I lost consciousness.

Dr. Markmann performed the operation in the way Dr. Naji had described. He inserted a camera and instruments through holes in my midriff, detached my left kidney by cutting the single ligament that held it on, caught it in the butterfly net and pulled it out through a three-inch cut below my belly button. No open procedure was necessary with its long incision around my torso. My kidney floated easily into the net and all went perfectly.

I had imagined before the surgery that after Dr. Markmann caught my kidney in the butterfly net, he would place it on a silver platter. Not on a stainless steel tray, which was what it probably wound up on, but on an ornate sterling silver platter with braided silver handles and a beautiful engraved "S" in the center so as to distinguish it from the other kidneys caught in their respective butterfly nets that day. And then I realized that the tray I was imagining was the tray that held my parents' elegant silver tea service, a wedding gift from a wealthy relative. The tea service was my mother's pride and joy. It was always polished. It was always on the buffet in the dining room, the centerpiece of the room.

One day when I was in college and I called home, I could tell that something was wrong. It took me a long time to wring the truth out of my mother. "Joan, we have been robbed." Well, actually technically, in the true legal sense, they hadn't been robbed at all since robbery is a theft involving some forceful taking directly from the person. Calling a "burglary," which involves breaking and entering when no one is home, a "robbery" is a common mistake made by lay people unschooled in the criminal law. That aside, my mother was distraught. Many of her prize possessions had been taken from the house when she and my father were on one of their rare Saturday nights out. They came home to find the front door lock jimmied. The first thing that my mother noticed was that her precious silver tea set was gone. When they went upstairs they noticed that much of my mother's antique gold jewelry had been lifted. They had taken her first tiny engagement ring, my father's mother's ring. They had left her stash of ancient cameos. She was relieved about that since they were irreplaceable. They had ignored my jewelry, even my gold charm bracelet. Luckily, my mother's diamond jewelry had either been on my mother's fingers or, as she would say, "in the vault." Most people would call it the safe deposit box.

A few weeks later when I called home my mother again sounded depressed. "What's wrong?" I asked.

"They came back."

"Who?"

"The robbers."

"What did they get this time?"

"Your charm bracelet is gone. So are my cameos."

I thought of the gaudy bracelet with the gold charms that I had collected during my adolescence, with replicas of the Eiffel Tower, a merry-go-round, a Ferris wheel, and a teddy bear. It also held cylindrical charms to celebrate the many Jewish passages of my youth, one emblazoned with the Star of David, a second with a menorah and the third with the Hebrew letter for life. I hadn't worn the bracelet for years yet I was still sad about its loss. And then I remembered my most prized possessions; well they weren't really my possessions but my father's. "What about daddy's medals, the ones from pharmacy school?"

"They didn't take those."

I heaved a sigh of relief. I was proud that I had always hidden with great care the gold metals my dad had won for being first in his pharmacy school class after I played with them as a child. I loved to take them out of their purple velvet container and look at them carefully. I marveled that my dad had won The Procter Prize, named after the father of American pharmacy, in spite of the long hours he had to work to put himself through school.

"They didn't take my compact either, the one that daddy gave me when we got engaged."

I didn't have the heart to tell her that it was unlikely that burglars who knew what they were doing—and these obviously did, since they came back twice when they saw that the little house in Oxford Circle contained a treasure trove of gold and silver— would have wanted the clunky faux gold and silver compact.

And so the silver tray from the tea set was not really lost to our family. It had been resurrected in my fantasy to bear the most precious gift I could ever give to anyone, my left kidney.

Dana, Darrah or Diana
and the Recovery Room

I awoke in the recovery room with searing pain in my left side. The pain lasted only a few minutes, thanks to the recovery room nurse who was either named Dana or Darrah. I was still very groggy when she introduced herself. "Hi. My name is Dana (or Darrah, it might have even been Diana). You're in the recovery room. I'll be your nurse. Let me know if you need more morphine."

"I need more morphine," I said without skipping a beat.

Most of the time I hate drugs that make me groggy, but I was in excruciating pain and the drug eased my pain immediately. I spent the rest of my time in the recovery room chatting with Dana or whatever her name was. I remember her as being petite, beautiful and friendly. I don't know if any of these assessments of her are true. What I did know was that I was in staggering pain and she was my supplier and she looked beautiful to me. She said that she was single but I couldn't figure out why. I'm not sure if that was true or just part of my morphine dream and my dependence on her to keep the morphine coming. I told her in my very high state that if I met anyone who was appropriate for her I would let her know. It would be interesting to know what else recovery room nurses are promised by their patients, grateful for the fixes they provide. In the few hours that Dana or Darrah and I spent together, I thought we had become fast friends.

My chats with Dana were punctuated with doctor visits. The first visit was from my Dr. King. Dr. Barnett came by too, but I don't think we talked any more about her childhood in Zimbabwe. Dr. Markmann looked in on me. Dr. Schwartz, the kindly endocrinologist without benefit of cell phone and my contemporary from Northeast Philadelphia, came by to see me. I was both surprised and delighted to see him. I had, after all, only consulted him one time. He apologized for not coming to see me before the surgery. He got to my room at 6:00 a.m. but I was already gone. He was on his way out of town and he came by to see me in recovery before he got on the plane.

My friend Billie and I hatched a plan before the surgery. Since we knew that John wouldn't be able to come see me in the recovery room, being otherwise actively engaged in surgery of his own, we decided that for the purposes of the hospital stay she would be my sister. The fact that our names were completely different would raise no questions, since women regularly take their husband's names. Neither of us had done that but we figured that the hospital staff would be none the wiser. Billie also had my power of attorney and had the right to pull any plug I might acquire during my hospitalization. And so Billie came into the recovery room and kissed me on the cheek. She was crying. She really was my sister. At the time I didn't appreciate the poignancy of her tears. The morphine had taken hold. I was feeling no pain and no emotion either.

Billie left, and Dana told me that John had just been brought to the recovery room and was doing well. I was surprised that he was already out of surgery. I sensed no passage of time from the moment I was brought into the recovery room until John was brought in, probably hours later.

I learned later that at about 9:00 or 10:00 a.m. Dr. Naji came to get John and brought him to the operating room. Dr. Naji didn't want to wait for an orderly, so he found a wheelchair and wheeled John to the operating theater himself. The kindly surgeon stopped on the way to chat with and introduce John to other physicians, including Dr. Rhoads, the energetic ninety-year-old surgeon in whose honor the building where our operations took place was named. After my kidney was removed, John's surgery began and likely lasted for some time after mine ended. Dana said that they would wheel me past John when I was carted back to my room. That sounded like a good idea to me, but I was still caught up in a morphine haze and likely would have thought almost anything Dana suggested was a good idea as long as she kept that morphine flowing.

At last it was time for me to leave the recovery room. As promised I was wheeled by John on my way out. He was a wonderful sight. His face was pink. No more ghostlike pallor. Could it be that my kidney was already working? It seemed like a miracle. I, who had always been sad that I had never given birth to a child, was for the first time and in a unique way giving life to someone I already loved.

MORPHINE ISN'T ALL IT'S CRACKED UP TO BE

Next thing I knew I was back in my room with what seemed to be casts of thousands. Billie and Bonnie were there, as were John's and my friends Jay and Janis. Billie saw the panic in my eyes. "Do you want everyone to leave?" she whispered in my ear.

"Please," I begged.

Everyone left. Bonnie and Billie came back a few minutes later. Jay and Janis went to John's room to wait for him to return. I felt guilty that I had asked them to go, since they had waited for us to come out of surgery all day. I just couldn't handle all of those people at one time.

I was not in much pain, I thought because of the morphine. I felt my left leg tightening and then loosening. It felt a little like the pressure of a cat resting on my calf. I worried that my nerves had gone dead in my right leg because I didn't feel the same tightening and loosening there. Nothing seemed very urgent because I remained in my recovery room stupor. Billie got me some ice chips, noticed that the morphine drip was not attached to my intravenous line and called the nurse. She told the nurse about the drip and about the pressure socks on my calves. Only one of them was working. That was why I had the catlike pressure in one leg but not two. Both socks are supposed to be in place to decrease the risk of phlebitis, so no errant blood clot can form in the legs after surgery, break off and rush to the heart, lungs or brain with catastrophic results. The morphine drip had to be attached to my body so that I could control the pain with a flick of the finger. The morphine accessibility was also important because apparently healing goes faster when there is good pain management. I had always heard that it was crucial to have advocates with you in the hospital. I never realized how important it was until my advocates needed to correct two important problems within one half hour of my arriving from the recovery room.

Billie and Bonnie checked on John for me and said that he seemed to be doing fine. They asked me if I wanted them to stay. I told them to go home. I didn't think that anything more could go wrong that night. I just wanted to sleep. I didn't feel half bad, having gone through a day's worth of surgery and recovery. And then I started to itch. It was the kind of itch I remember having in my last few years of eating shellfish, just before the allergy caused me to stop breathing. I called for the nurse. She told me the itching could be from the morphine and that she would get in touch with one of the residents and see if they could change the drip to another drug. That sounded fine to me, and I thought that I remembered that at sometime during the night the drip was changed. Still I felt itchy. To prove the rusty adage "A little knowledge is a dangerous thing," I decided that I was having an anaphylactic reaction to the morphine and to whatever drug was substituted for it, and that after the itching would come an inability to breathe. Just like what happened with the mussels and shrimp scampi when I was twenty-five. I decided that it would be safer to stay up all night so that if the itching morphed into trouble breathing I could quickly hit the nurse panic button and get help.

I stayed awake all night and was wide-awake when the Dr. Markmann came to see me at the crack of dawn. "How are you doing?"

"Fine except for the itching."

"It could be from the morphine."

"No, they changed that in the middle of the night," I assured him. He came over to look at the drip. I looked at it for the first time. It was the first time it was light enough to see it.

"It is still morphine," the surgeon said.

Just after he left, a nurse came in and disconnected the drip from my arm. Percocet came next for pain control.

Then I left messages for my friends to thank each of them for their support and to tell them how wonderful I felt. I still must have been a little high. This telling the world that I was doing okay must have been some bizarre offshoot of my mother's training that you should always send a thank-you note immediately upon receiving a gift. So, there to greet my friends as they arrived at work (it was much too early to call them at home) was my much too cheery voice telling them that everything was fine. I'm sure that they weren't expecting that quite so soon and were suspicious. They were correct to be suspicious because I was still roped to a catheter and still had not even tried to get out of bed.

I spoke to John that morning too, by phone. Both of us were still bedridden. He seemed to be doing well, but not as well as I was. I just rationalized, "He's a man and much more sensitive to pain." Dr. Naji told us when we first met him that ordinarily when he couldn't find a transplant recipient that they would be in the donor's room. We assured him it would be just the opposite with us.

Dr. Grossman came in to tell me that John's creatinine was 1.7 and mine was 1.2, just what they had expected. To me it meant that both of my kidneys were working fine.

They told me that my catheter would be removed in the afternoon. I was resistant to the idea of having one in the first place, but Dr. Naji assured me that I would be happy to have it in the first day after the operation. Happy I was. Getting out of bed was not something I was eager to do. The catheter was removed. When I did get out of bed I was hunched over and inched my way to the bathroom, which in "The Four Seasons Room" was only a few feet from the bed. It hurt both to walk and to maneuver my body around in the bathroom. Then I decided that rather than going back to bed that I should hobble over to the upholstered wing chair and sit there for a while. While I was sitting in the chair, our friends from Washington, D.C., Tom and Joan, walked in. They were surprised to see me up and about. They had just come from John's room. He was lying in bed, still attached to his catheter, and he was not ready to walk or sit in a chair. Joan had the remnants of a cold and a surgical mask covered her face. It made talking with her a little surreal. I was grateful for the bagels they brought. It was my first real food. I still hadn't touched any of the hospital fare.

Dr. Naji came in later, trailed by residents and medical students. After inquiring about my health, he asked, "What's different about John?"

"His color," I said. Dr. Naji beamed. It was obviously the right answer.

Toward evening I hobbled down to John's room. I had to lean on the rail along the wall and shuffle down the hallway. John's room was only four doors away from mine and I arrived eventually. It was great to see John. I had missed him. His color was still pink. He was in pain. His incision was much larger than mine. He told me that the extreme fatigue he had endured for the last few months was gone. While I was in the room I met John's nurse Joanne, a sometimes-gruff drill-sergeant kind of person, tough as nails on the outside but warm at heart. Joanne was explaining John's myriad drugs to him. I stayed to listen for a while and then I realized that I had to urinate. I told Joanne that I was going back to my room because I was worried about John's compromised immune system, afraid I would contaminate him if I used his bathroom. "You're his wife and don't want to use his bathroom? You'll have to get over that," she said with a look that showed the folly of my extreme infection precautions.

During the evening shift one of the nurses gave me a "hug me" pillow to hold against my stomach so my newly arranged insides wouldn't rattle when I walked. It worked, along with the occasional Percocet. When I took my evening stroll to John's room, his ebullient night nurse had made him a "hug me" pillow emblazoned with Christmas trees and candy canes. Now John has no love for Christmas, mainly because his father died on Christmas day. Nevertheless, he adored his "hug me" pillow that helped take away the pain. We made it through our first postoperative day. Both of us felt okay. We expected we would only feel better the next day.

Recovery

Just when I thought that recovery from major surgery was a piece of cake came the second day after surgery. I awoke feeling horrible. I was nauseated, bloated and exhausted. I had gas pains from my throat to my stomach and in my shoulders. The surgical resident came in and told me if I wanted I could leave the hospital that day. I wasn't even sure that I could leave my bed that day. Since I felt worse than I ever remember feeling, I declined. Part of my dressing was taken off, revealing huge brownish-red burns caused by the bandages. I was the victim of yet another allergy to join the one to shellfish. Now I was allergic to adhesive. I was assured that the burns would go away. I wasn't too concerned with how my abdomen looked cosmetically. With the bright red puncture wounds on my stomach, my bikini days seemed to be over anyway.

This time John came to my room, as Dr. Naji said he would. Now I knew why. Dr. Naji knew how I would be feeling two days after surgery. Bonnie, who had also had laparoscopic abdominal surgery, had told me well before I went into the hospital that she had had horrible pain in the shoulder, chest and abdomen, pain no one had warned her about. Apparently the pain is from the carbon dioxide that is pumped into the abdomen to make the operative field bigger. When I awoke feeling great the day after surgery I thought that somehow I had dodged the carbon dioxide bullet. On the second postoperative day I knew that I hadn't.

I was given a stool softener to clear the way for the much-awaited post-surgical bowel movement. I took myself off of Percocet, which is notorious for causing constipation. I changed to my old reliable, Tylenol, which I knew had no adverse side effects taken in moderation. I must admit that I craved it on day two in more than moderation. The nurses kept a strict ration on the Tylenol, its having fairly recently been shown to cause liver damage in large quantities. Since I had grown up in a drugstore I had always been very wary of taking any kind of drug. My experience with morphine and Percocet only reinforced my father's warnings about drugs. His view was that you're better off without them.

By that evening, I had expelled enough gas to make me feel better. I ventured off to visit John in his room and in a burst of energy—perhaps the gas spurred me on—I circled the Christmas tree at the end of the hall and then doubled back to John's room. John announced that he had talked with The Girl with the Hat and he had told her that he wouldn't have anything more to do with her because it upset me so much. It only took my giving him a vital organ to have the motivation to say goodbye. I thanked him, but I was skeptical about how long his resolve would last. I kissed John and went back to my room for a nap.

When I went to visit John later that night, I had a fight on my hands. John was due to get his anti-rejection drugs at 8:00

p.m. Not yet experienced with the nuances of the scheduling of those drugs, I assumed that they needed to be given at 8:00 p.m. on the dot. I went to the nurse's station at 8:15 and told the nurse on duty, not our by-now-beloved Joanne but an unfriendly, seemingly unconcerned dour woman who took her place, that John hadn't had his 8:00 p.m. dose of medicine. "I'll get around to it," she said. By 9:00 p.m. she still hadn't come with the medicine and I asked her again. She didn't look busy. She was talking with one of the other nurses. Still nothing happened. Now I was really worried. I decided to try again.

"When will you give my husband his medicine?" She looked at me. She was annoyed. "When is the latest he can get it so that there is no problem?"

"As long as he gets it by 10:00 it will be all right."

"It is 10:15."

A few minutes later she was in the room with the immuno-suppressants. I don't know what would have happened if I hadn't been there to pester her. So now I was not only being an advocate for my husband but also an advocate for my own kidney. I hadn't gone through all of this physical pain and emotional turmoil to have some incompetent nurse foul up his anti-rejection medication. The medicine was necessary to keep John's body from rejecting the foreign body, my kidney, which had been implanted just a few days earlier. While anti-rejection medicine does not need to be given at precisely the exact time it is due, it must be given within a certain time window, especially when the transplant is new. That is the time that the body is most likely to reject a foreign organ. That nurse could be lackadaisical when it came to someone else's organs, but I was going to be damned if I would let her be lazy when it came to John and me.

Each patient in the hospital needs an advocate, even in as good a place as the University of Pennsylvania Medical Center.

For the transplant patient, getting his or her medication on time is crucial for the survival of the transplanted organ. Without an advocate, the patient is at the mercy of the nurse. Although most of the transplant nurses adhere scrupulously to the medication schedule, every once in a while a nurse will need to be prodded.

The next day Dr. Naji came by with his entourage. "We're going to operate on her tomorrow," he kidded.

"No way," I laughed, "you had your chance."

I was proud that I had recovered so well. I felt like a poster girl for the laparoscopic procedure. I might even recover more quickly than my friend Jeanne in the competition that she didn't even know that she was a part of.

John called to ask me to come to his room to meet Ellen Markmann. She was the sister-in-law of my surgeon, Dr. Markmann, who had three brothers and a sister. Two of his brothers were surgeons and one was an accountant. Dr. Markmann's sister married Dr. Naji. A family that transplants together.....
When I arrived at John's room, Mrs. Markmann had about twenty vials of pills and capsules lined up on a table. She went through each one, explained what it was for and the dosage. She told us it wouldn't be necessary to memorize all of it. The discharge summary would have the instructions. She just wanted us to become somewhat familiar with the drugs. It was all very confusing to both of us, even me, the pharmacist's daughter. We were both exhausted from surgery and, because of anesthesia or stress, our minds weren't working well. I decided that the responsibility for the drugs would be John's and not mine. After all, I had just given him my kidney. The least he could do was to take responsibility for keeping it. That was an unusual attitude on my part, because I regularly helped John with his medication before the transplant. It was also odd because as a pharmacist's daughter I was familiar with medications and dosages. I was tired out from

the surgery and didn't want any further responsibilities. It was enough to contemplate going home.

Both John and I had a lot of trepidation about going home where there was no one to take care of us. The fact that there had been no one hired even for a few days had been my fault. I just wouldn't allow myself to think that we would be so disabled that we would need someone. I did ask Bonnie to bring us dinner and stay over on Friday night, Maureen on Saturday night. I just hoped that it would be enough.

Our discharge instructions gave me even more pause. We were only supposed to climb one to two flights of stairs per day. We were not supposed to carry anything that weighed more than ten pounds. And we lived in a four-story house. It was possible to do most of what we had to do on two floors. The floor with the kitchen and the dining room did not have a bathroom, so after Bonnie and Maureen left, climbing a flight of stairs several times per day would be necessary. We weren't really sure how we were going to do that without violating our instructions.

Our friend Millie, a cardiac nurse, came to take us home. Two of the nurse's aides helped us into wheelchairs and wheeled us to the hospital entrance. We slowly got into Millie's car. We felt every pothole, and there were many of them, between our house and the hospital. Millie drove slowly and carefully, but every tiny bump resonated through our bodies.

We were so happy when we arrived home to our house and our cats. Millie left after getting us settled. Then we were alone and frightened. We slowly made our way up the stairs to our bedroom. We knew we would be there most of the time for the next few days. The doorbell rang. I went halfway down the stairs and screamed, I think a little desperately, "Who's there?" I had to go all the way down for a package. I realized that I had used up all of my one to two flights for the day and the day was young. The stairs were the toughest. With every stair came a shaking of my insides. I yearned for a one-floor apartment just for a few weeks.

When I opened the package, I realized that The Girl with the Hat had struck again. She had been the reason for my unnecessary trek down the stairs. She had sent each of us a book and a note. I quickly dumped both my note and my book in the trash, without looking at either. I had never thrown a book away before, but this seemed like the appropriate first time. I gave John his book and his note. I don't know what he did with them. I told him what I thought he should do with them, which was different from dispatching them to the trash. I realized that his resolution not to contact his old friend because it upset me wouldn't last long.

Soon after we arrived home I called Isabelle and Didier. Isabelle answered. "I was worried about you all day on December 14," she said. It turned out she had her own concerns that day. About the same time that we were having our operations her daughter Juliette was born by Caesarean section. She and the baby were doing fine. We marveled at the coincidence. Juliette was born on the same day and at the same time that John got a new lease on life. We knew that both of our families would always cherish December 14, 1999, as a date that changed all of our lives.

After our talk with Isabelle, we drifted off into one of our deep sleep naps. Somehow anesthesia stays in the body for a long time, stored in fat cells of which I had quite a few at the time. John's fat cells were getting more numerous by the minute as the prednisone he was taking to stop rejection made him ravenous. Sleeps and naps after general anesthesia are profoundly deep, apparently because little bits of anesthesia break free of the fat cells and circulate.

I noticed that John was becoming very testy. I was miffed, somehow expecting that he would be so grateful for my having given him a kidney that he would no longer be moody or cranky as he sometimes was before the operations. He had had a minimum of cranky episodes in the last year but now I wondered if that was to butter me up so that I would give him the kidney. Actually, I found out later, some of John's anti-rejection drugs caused mood swings.

John was handling his drugs himself. I worried about that because at times he seemed confused, also a consequence of some of the drugs. The directions for taking the medication on the discharge summary were confusing because of the volume of drugs he had to take and the differing dosages. I would hear him talking out loud and becoming very frustrated as he was trying to figure out what drugs to take when.

When I asked him if he needed help, he would yell "no." I didn't press him for fear that he would snap at me again. I just let him deal with the medication himself even though I heard him say, "I'm not sure if I took this before," and "Did I take that yesterday?" I wondered if he was taking the correct drug at the right time. I just didn't have the energy or the nerve to try to help.

THE "R" WORD

John had to return to the Transplant Clinic the Monday after the operation for blood tests. He worried for days whether the taxi driver would be able to find our street. Finding our block has never been easy, since it is tucked away amid a group of one-way streets and unless you know exactly where you are going, the street can elude you. We were victims of the inability to find the street soon after we signed an agreement of sale on the house. We had just had dinner with friends in the neighborhood of our new purchase, wanted to show them our new home and found that we couldn't find South American Street. Here we had forked over thousands of dollars for a down payment and our house was lost.

When we had our surgeries, our house was even more difficult to locate because the street sign for American Street had been missing for months, the victim of a Philadelphia Gas Works truck stymied by the sharp turn. Now all that remained was the earlier name of the street, Ashland, etched in stone on one of the houses. So, as far as any cab driver or anyone else for that matter was concerned, there was no American Street, only Ashland. Ordinarily, it didn't really matter if a cab couldn't find us because we could find one on the street about a block away. Now there was no way John could imagine walking one block. I wanted to offer to go with him but I just couldn't bring myself to do that. I was too tired. When I called the cab company and scrupulously gave directions to a bored operator, I told her that John had just had surgery, hoping that she would send a driver who didn't think the potholes were daring him to drive over them.

The taxi arrived. John hobbled down the steps to the cab. He didn't return home until several hours later, after having waited a long time to see the doctor and to have a blood test. John's blood pressure was still high, which frightened both of us since high blood pressure was listed in the book that the Transplant Clinic gave us as being a harbinger of rejection, the dreaded "R" word. Now came the waiting, something John had been used to, since he waited in fear for almost thirty years each time he had a blood test to see how high his creatinine levels had risen. For me the waiting was a relatively new phenomenon. Now I was waiting to see how my kidney was doing. Somehow it felt like a test of my own value. Was my kidney good enough?

Finally, after being home a few hours, John talked to one of the transplant coordinators. Apparently his creatinine was much higher than it had been in the hospital only a few days before, another indication of the dreaded rejection. I felt like I had in junior high when the popular girls were mean to me and the boys ignored me, and like I had at the Girard College social in high school when even the orphans wouldn't give me the time of day. I felt like all of me was being rejected, not just my kidney.

We had hoped that John would sail easily through this post-operative period without any complications. Now one of the worst possible complications was staring us in the face. If John's body rejected the kidney, our operations would have been for naught, and I would have to, for no good reason, finish out my life with only one kidney instead of two. We had hoped that John would have been one of the transplant patients in the clinic waiting room who bragged about never having had an episode of rejection in the two, five, ten or twenty years since transplant surgery. John didn't have those bragging rights for more than a few days. We might be facing an episode of rejection in less than one week after the transplant. For both of us, who had rarely received anything less than an A, this early problem felt like a profound failure.

John was told to drink a lot of water, to eat a lot of salt and to return to the Transplant Clinic the next day for more blood tests. The doctors thought he might be dehydrated, which could make his creatinine levels appear higher than they actually were. John drank quarts of water, ate bags of potato chips and returned to the Clinic on Tuesday, exactly one week after the surgery. This time I went with him. I was somehow sure that we were staring rejection in the face, that John was rejecting my kidney as somehow unworthy. This time the blood test was done as soon as we arrived, and the results were reported immediately. The nephrologists and the kidney team were not around. Tuesday was liver transplant day. The heptologists were in, the nephrologists out. Dr. Grossman was called from his office to the Clinic to talk with John.

"It is almost certainly rejection," Dr. Grossman told us. "First, we have to rule out structural problems with the graft." They had to rule out the possibility that the kidney hadn't been properly implanted in John's body. John had to have a renal scan first and then had to be readmitted to the fourth floor of the Rhoads Building. All I could think of was that there was something wrong with my kidney and if John had received a kidney from The Girl with the Hat or The Little Redheaded Girl, maybe everything would be all right. Setbacks like this one always made me feel just like I did when I was being criticized by my mother or taunted by the popular girls in seventh grade. I could never measure up. Now even my kidney couldn't measure up and that was why we were back in the Rhoads Building—not bragging about the fact that there had been no rejection for years, but with my failure of a kidney that couldn't even make it for a week without being rejected.

I also felt angry with John. I somehow knew for the last few days that John wasn't paying enough attention to his medication. He was adamant that I not interfere with the medicines. How do you get a gift like that, a kidney for God's sake, and squander it?

Going back to Rhoads 4 was not a triumphal return. It felt like a terrible defeat. Before a bed could be found for John we were placed in a room with other failures, other people who were rejecting their newly implanted organs. The transplant floor was full. It was December 21. Christmas carols were playing everywhere, and car crashes and suicides provided organs for people who had been eagerly awaiting new body parts for years.

Finally John got a room. Our dear Joanne was his nurse again. She and the doctors tried to reassure John by telling him that rejection episodes happen often and they sometimes see people back a few times. How much better to be those "no rejection" braggers! I didn't want John and my kidney to be the champion of many rejection episodes. The plan now was to stop the rejection and to send the creatinine downward. John's creatinine had risen in only a matter of days to 2.6. A massive dose of steroids was infused into his arm. There would be three such infusions. If they didn't work, there would need to be a biopsy and then perhaps more potent anti-rejection drugs. Again the wait for the blood test results. I went to the hospital cafeteria to get food for both of us for lunch and dinner. It was apparent to me from our first hospital stay that no one could survive on the hospital food, let alone get better and stronger. John's appetite had become ravenous, a side effect of prednisone, the steroid he was taking to prevent rejection. John not only ate the hospital food. He also ate the gigantic turkey sandwiches I brought him from the cafeteria. Other side effects of the huge doses of steroids that John received intravenously were confusion and hallucinations. Even the smaller amounts of prednisone that John took when he first left the hospital, I learned during the second hospital stay, can lead to mood swings and disorientation. And I was letting a confused guy in the first days after a transplant operation dole out his own pills.

When I looked at the new transplant recipients and donors hobbling down the hall, I could hardly believe that I had been that disabled the week before. I stayed at the hospital until 10:00 p.m. that night. I kept trying to get the results of the renal scan but they weren't available. It was easier to stay in the hospital where there were no stairs to climb than to go home where the three flights were formidable. John gave me a list of things he wanted from home. I drew the line at his laptop.

When I returned from the hospital, I spoke with some of my friends. At first I was ashamed to tell them that John was experiencing a rejection episode and that my kidney was being rejected. It felt like a romantic rejection, like a failure. Not that I wasn't used to romantic rejections. My life had been peppered with them. They were never easy for me to deal with. My kidney was a failure and by a strange kind of guilt by association, so was I.

John called me from the hospital the next morning. "My creatinine came down from 2.6 to 2.5." It didn't seem like much to

John or me but Dr. Grossman said to John, "I'll take it." I suppose that any indication that the creatinine wasn't continuing to go up was good. The renal scan was normal. It was rejection and, of all things, we were relieved that it wasn't any of the other possibilities that might have required another surgery. Not only was it rejection, but the first intravenous shot of steroids seemed to get the rejection somewhat under control.

I came to the hospital later that morning. I wasn't supposed to lift anything heavy after the surgery. I was bringing all of the things John asked for—toiletries, pajamas, a robe. I was also schlepping dozens of sandwiches and loads of cookies one of our friends dropped off at the house. I had no trouble getting a cab. My troubles began when I got to the hospital. I don't know why I didn't go into the Rhoads entrance I had used many times before. Because it was cold, I went into the hospital entrance just across the street from where the cab let me off. I knew that the packages that I was carrying were too heavy for me. I just figured that I would be at my destination before I knew it and wouldn't do any permanent damage. When I arrived in the hospital lobby I asked directions to the Rhoads Building. I got the wrong directions. I found myself wandering for what seemed like hours but probably wasn't any more than twenty minutes. I looked for open offices on my way. Most of the offices were closed since people were off on their Christmas holidays. I didn't know what to do. My stomach was killing me. The bags felt heavier. I asked for directions again. The person I asked had no idea where Rhoads was and made no effort to help me find out. I'm sure that she saw the pain in my eyes but didn't seem to care. I always thought that if people chose to work in a hospital that they would be automatically sympathetic. Why would someone who doesn't care about other people choose to work in a place that should be devoted to alleviating others' pain? I wandered aimlessly through hallways and kept facing dead ends. I put down my bags in the middle of the hallway and started to cry. I just didn't think that I could go on. Then I saw it, the Department of Surgery. Someone was in the library there and directed me to my destination. It wasn't far. I made it. When I arrived at the transplant wing, one of the nurses helped me carry my bundles to John's room. I didn't want John to know what I had gone through. I brushed the tears away before I entered his room and smiled when I saw him.

When I arrived at John's room I didn't realize right away that he had gone for a shave and a haircut. Joanne had urged him to go to the hospital barber. On the way he stopped at the gift shop, and bought me a stuffed basset hound that we named "Sweetie Pie," a name John often said he called me so as to avoid accidentally calling me by the name of one of his ex-wives or of The Girl with the Hat.

When the doctors arrived on rounds later in the day one of the senior physicians explained the rejection process to us and to the more junior doctors. "Rejection," he explained, "is a cellular process." The cells from John's body were attacking the transplanted kidney, my kidney.

And then I had an idea. I had heard of visualization. I didn't know exactly what it was or how to do it. From what I had heard it was usually something an ill person did to stem a disease in his or her own body. Here was my idea. The kidney until very recently had been mine. I figured that I had a right to practice visualization or whatever I wanted with it. I mentioned visualization to John and he didn't seem interested. So I took matters into my own hands. I visualized my kidney with two arms, one on each end. Then I started to use the kidney's fists to punch at the cells that were invading it.

When I told my friend Jeanne about my visualization experiment and mentioned my kidney's hitting at the invading cells with its fists; she said she had an idea. Jeanne, being an artist and more expert at things visual than I, who could do no better than a D in high school art, suggested that as long as I was doing this visualizing, why didn't I put boxing gloves on the kidney's fists to make them more powerful? And so I did. Now my kidney had strapped on her gloves and was punching out the lights of those invading cells. It seemed even more effective when I closed my eyes, visualized the invading cells, thought of the kidney and used my own arms sans boxing gloves to bat out the marauding cells.

John was told Wednesday night that he would be awakened at the crack of dawn on Thursday, blood would be drawn and a decision would be made whether or not to perform the biopsy and go on to the more potent anti-rejection drugs. The reason for all of the early morning activity was that Christmas was fast approaching with its vacations and skeleton staff and, if necessary, the biopsy had to be done right away.

I was eager to find out the results of the Thursday 5:00 a.m. blood test but my hands were tied. I couldn't call the hospital until 8:15 a.m. John called me. His creatinine was 2.1. He would get one more infusion and then he could come home. The boxing gloves had worked. Either the boxing gloves or the steroids or both. Friends brought John home. When he arrived, his arm was swollen to twice its normal size. Apparently the steroid had gone into the muscle in his arm instead of into his blood stream where it belonged. I was terribly afraid that that meant that the steroid had not gone where it was supposed to go and that we would be back in the room with the rest of the failures before we knew it.

Now we played a waiting game again until Monday, when John would go back to the clinic for his next phlebotomist's stab and another long wait for blood test results. This time I told John that I was taking over the distribution of the medicines. Getting the twenty-something pills a day organized was complicated even for a pharmacist's daughter with two advanced degrees and a background in medical malpractice law. For a transplant patient unfamiliar with the pills and dosages and in a confused post-surgical state, getting the pills right without aid was nearly impossible. The only way that I could manage the pills was to use a container for each day that had four compartments, one compartment each for dosages before breakfast, with breakfast, at lunchtime and at bedtime. Even then I had to refer again and again to the dosage instructions.

Over the next weekend I found that I could do more—simple meal preparation, even the laundry, emptying the dishwasher. I never thought that I could enjoy those tasks so much. I was so happy to be getting almost back to normal. I even called a client to make an appointment for the first week of January. The independence and self-sufficiency I feared that I would lose forever was coming back. I graduated to more flights of stairs per day. The pieces of bandage held on by my dissolving stitches began to fall away to reveal what looked like raw cat scratches on my midriff and below my belly button. The adhesive burns were disappearing. My energy was returning, but too many stairs or too much exertion made me feel very tired. I still took naps that brought me to the deepest sleep I had ever experienced. All in all, though, I felt like I was on the mend.

John, on the other hand, was cranky and sometimes downright nasty. He kept blaming it on the drugs. In fact some of the drugs he was taking alter mood, but I thought that it was more than that. Not only did I want a divorce, but I thought I had been foolish to give this ungrateful wretch my kidney. I should have given it to some Nobel Prize contender. I mainly wished that John's state of intense crabbiness would end.

Monday came. John went for his blood tests. All weekend I had been furiously doing my boxing exercises on the visualized kidney. I kept my fingers crossed all day that the boxing kidney had worked, or that something had worked. I met John at Tiffany's on his way back from the hospital. He bought me a tiny gold Elsa Peretti bean. Actually it looks just like a kidney. It was my substitute for the real thing. I vowed never to take it off. Other women might have wanted a three-carat diamond for such a sacrifice but the kidney bean was fine with me. The blood test results came back. The creatinine was still down. John was told to come back to the Clinic the following Thursday. We went out to lunch to celebrate. Only the finest for us, Pizzeria Uno. It was the closest restaurant to our house. Just two blocks away. How exciting to go out to a restaurant and be waited on. When we arrived home we were exhausted.

We had weathered our first, and hopefully our last, episode of rejection. In commemoration of our victory, we decided to give John and my kidney a name. We chose Sydney Kidney. We thought it had a nice ring to it. I thought she should have a middle name and so she became Sydney Joan Kidney, the lovely demure vital organ who, when she needed to, could strap on her boxing gloves and knock the lights out of any and all attacking cells.

Recuperation and the Faux Millennium

We had a goal, or at least I had one since well before the operation, to make it to the New Year 2000 concert at the Academy of Music, the home of the Philadelphia Orchestra. Most of our friends had more ambitious plans for what was a faux millennium (the real beginning of the millennium was 2001)—trips to exotic locales, black tie parties. I just wanted John and I to be able to leave the house for a few hours two weeks after each of us had major surgery. I bought the tickets in November, hoping we would be able to use them. I knew that if we weren't up to it I could pass them on to someone else. I knew that they were there in the bureau drawer in the bedroom. I focused on them in my darkest hours of imaginary pounding on my visualized kidney.

When both of us were out of the hospital by December 18, I thought that the concert was a real possibility. I don't think that I cared much about the concert itself. It was Barbara Cook and the

Philadelphia Orchestra. I had always wanted to see Cook in person, since she was the singer I had listened to as a teenager on the original cast album of "The Music Man" and because she specialized in the songs of two of my favorite lyricists, Oscar Hammerstein—whose home we had come dangerously close to buying in the weeks before the transplant—and Stephen Sondheim. The real goal was for John and me to go out with some degree of independence. Because of John's return to the hospital on December 22, he was pessimistic about whether he could make it to the orchestra or back to teach in mid-January. I, ever the optimist, hoped that he could do both. The New Year's concert was a symbol for me of both healing and renewed independence.

We were both concerned about navigating the twelve blocks between our house and the Academy of Music, the grand old building where the concert would be held. The Academy is such a perfect example of a nineteenth-century opera house that Martin Scorsese himself chose it as the centerpiece in pivotal scenes in *The Age of Innocence.* We were not too happy about the prospect of taking yet another cab ride. Even the most careful taxi driver could not avoid the bumping that caused pain in our relatively new incisions.

At the last minute we steeled ourselves and decided to give it a try. We donned our Cannes finery. What we didn't realize was how difficult it would be to get it on. John put on his tux very gingerly. It was not easy for me to help him with his cummerbund and suspenders, but I managed to do so without inflicting much pain on either of us. My dressing was even more of a problem. I had to put my dress over my head. It was the first time I had tried that maneuver since the surgery. I had only worn dresses that buttoned down the front or pants, skirts and blouses that could easily be pulled up. I felt a stab of pain in my incision as I lifted my arms up and pulled the dress on. But then the pain subsided and I was dressed quite nicely for a woman who was still convalescing. We grabbed a cab about a half block from home. The cab driver gently squired us to the Academy.

The Academy of Music looked especially beautiful to us that night. The elegant brick facade was lit by ancient gas lamps. Inside the reds of the velvet upholstery and the golds of the ubiquitous gilt trim were set off by thousands of white balloons trailing long white ribbons. At each seat was a silver bag with noisemakers, whistles and a split of champagne. Many of the men wore tails; some of the women wore dazzling gowns. The mood was festive. The orchestra played Copland and Bernstein, two of John's favorites. To my delight Barbara Cook sang some of my Hammerstein favorites. At midnight the orchestra played "Auld Lang Syne." The screen next to the stage showed the fireworks from Penn's Landing.

John and I knew at midnight that we had made it. We had a new year to look forward to. John had a new life to look forward to, a life of more energy, more hope, less dread. We kissed each other and floated out of the Academy. And then we were afraid.

There were hordes of people on the street, not only the people who poured out of the packed concert hall; revelers from all over town were converging on to Broad Street where the Academy is located. There were no taxis to be found. Apparently all of Philadelphia had heeded the warning not to drink and drive and had grabbed a cab. We were feeling very vulnerable and for good reason. Our incisions hurt. We were afraid of being jostled. Even our small cats jumping on the bed was more shaking than we could stand. We had banned them from our room since the surgeries. The idea of being pushed by an adult, even inadvertently, was more than we could handle. We were afraid of falling. And then out of the blue a fat purple tourist bus, the Philly Phlash, appeared on the corner where we were standing. The corner wasn't a bus stop but the light had turned red just as we hobbled there. The Phlash stopped. The driver must have seen the terror in our eyes. He opened the door and let us get on. We thanked him profusely. We were relieved.

From the bus we got a look at all of the people who, along with us, were ecstatic about the promise of a new year. We were thrilled too, especially because we were safely on our way home. Or were we? Suddenly I heard someone on the bus cough. Then he sneezed. Another cough. Another sneeze. He didn't bother to cover his nose and mouth. I had thought nothing of this before. A cold was no big deal. I had probably been guilty of not using a tissue as much as I should have. Now I thought that I could see and feel those droplets of liquid germs wafting in our direction and infecting John, whose compromised immune system could no longer easily fight off the common cold. I saw John stiffen as he heard the coughs and sneezes too, trying to steel himself against the approaching troops of germs.

As the bus approached our street, we saw battalions of people. When we stepped out only one-half block from home, we felt panicky and vulnerable again. Thousands of people were heading in our direction. We realized that they were coming from the Penn's Landing fireworks display, the same fireworks we had seen on screen at the Academy. We were afraid that we would be pushed or manhandled by some of the revelers who had had one or two too many to welcome in the New Year. We managed to avoid the bulk of the mass of humanity by ducking down a side street. We responded in kind to the shouts of "Happy New Year" that we heard all around us. And then we were home. Unscathed. Elated. Triumphant. We both began to think that everything would be all right.

Back to Our New Normal

A few days after our New Year's Eve excursion John went back for another blood test. We held our collective breaths. The results were good, really good. The creatinine was still down. John continued to be difficult to get along with and kept blaming the medication. I guessed that that was possible but it seemed to be more than that. He might have been worried about going back to school, worried if he had enough stamina to teach and worried if he could dodge his students' coughs and sneezes. The grumpier he acted the more I wondered if I should have given my kidney to some Nobel Laureate.

I went back to my office for the first time a little over two weeks after the operation. Well, maybe I couldn't beat my friend Jeanne at the recuperation game, but at least it was close. Sitting up all day proved exhausting. In the afternoon I met with a client in another lawyer's office. I didn't get home until after seven. I was exhausted, but I felt like getting back in the swim of things was a major accomplishment.

With the second shipment of John's drugs came a raft of papers detailing the side effects of the ten medications. Because John was prone to hypochondria I was happy that he put the sheaf of papers aside. I, on the other hand, picked up the papers and read all of the possible effects of the drugs he was forced to take, both to prevent rejection and to control high blood pressure. John had already begun to experience the mood swings, the hand tremors and cramping in his feet, legs and hands that the literature suggested were caused by the drugs.

Another blood test. We held our breath. Another good report.

About a month after our surgeries we got great news. Dr. Grossman told John that he didn't have to see him for a week. Sydney Joan Kidney was holding her own against the onslaught of the invading cells. The staples at John's incision were removed. His creatinine was at 1.4.

I went with John to the transplant clinic when he got his next blood test. I ran into Dr. Grossman in the hall and asked,. "Is John over the hump?"

"He'll never be over the hump, but he seems to be doing fine,." the doctor said.

Dr. Grossman also told me that day in the hall that it isn't much of a problem to identify rejection when the creatinine jumps suddenly. The rejections that are more difficult to diagnose are the ones where the creatinine creeps up slowly. Now I had something else to worry about, the creeping-up-slowly brand of rejection.

I couldn't seem to get it into my head that this roller coaster was a lifelong, or at least as long as John has my kidney, kind of thing. It isn't as if I wasn't warned about that by the social worker I talked to about kidney donation soon after I found out that we were a match. She had told me that transplant was not a cure for kidney disease but simply substituted new concerns for those of failing kidneys. I just had trouble believing what she said. I had convinced myself against all reason that as soon as I gave John my kidney everything would be all right. The transplant fairytale would have a happy ending. Getting the kidney at least in the short term prevented John from needing dialysis. We traded the problems of chronic kidney failure for the constant fear of rejection, a compromised immune system, the ever-present fear of infection and the often-difficult side effects of the immunosuppressant drugs.

Now it was my turn for follow-up with Dr. Naji. One side of my abdomen seemed to be fatter than the other. He told me that with time they would equalize. I don't know why I was being so vain about my stomach. The only person who ever saw my belly was John. After Dr. Naji examined me he gently helped me up from the table. "Dr. Naji, you don't fit the high-powered surgeon stereotype."

"We see life and death so closely, it doesn't make sense to be like that."

"Thanks for everything. Please thank Dr. Markmann for me."

"Of course."

School started for John in earnest in the middle of January. Now both of us were coming home exhausted. In retrospect, we both went back to work too soon. I think that it was mainly my fault that we did that. I guess I thought that if everything looked to be normal that it would be. John had far too many students in each of his classes. Rather than being flattering, it just meant more work. He had to reply to more e-mails begging for entry, listen to pleas for admittance in person and turn many people away. There were also queries about the Cannes program. The deadline for application was fast approaching. John, who has always prided himself in standing and moving around the room when he taught, had to teach his classes sitting down.

When I went back to work after that first time, I sat aimlessly at my office for hours at a time. I had successfully pushed almost everything off of my desk before the operation and nothing much had come in since. I did have several inquiries about medical malpractice cases. I referred them to another lawyer. I spent at least part of each day in the office napping on the couch. I pushed papers from one side of the desk to another. I became a champion of busywork because I was too tired to do anything else. I had every household and office bill paid days before they were due. That was the deepest thinking that I could bring myself to do. Anything that required the least bit of original thought was exceedingly difficult. I continued to have lingering anesthesia effects. There were those deep-sleep naps. Sometimes I couldn't summon up the precise word that I wanted to use. Before the operation, summoning up words was a piece of cake. I had trouble concentrating for more than a few minutes at a time. In my more lucid moments, of which there had been few in the month after the surgery, I wondered if my brain would ever be as good as it was in the beginning of December. Losing my sharp mind would be far worse than just losing my kidney.

In his first week back at work John had to attend an organizational meeting for a March conference. He was exhausted when he got home and he still had another day of teaching, another day of fielding a barrage of pleas to get into his courses. When he got home from work at the end of his first week back at school, he told me that he had run into one of the Penn administrators who asked how he and I were feeling. Our secret seemed to be out from an unexpected source, someone at Penn John thought he could trust to keep a confidence. I urged John to talk to the source of the gossip to try to stop it, but he was too exhausted to do so. I was infuriated by the leak because I didn't tell some close friends about the operation for fear that they would tell someone at Penn. I had given them the South Beach story and now they could find out the truth from a perfect stranger. Several of my friends who were in on our secret said that we should have expected the story to come out because, after all, it was such a good story, so much human interest. I wasn't really interested in the gossip value of our lives. I was more concerned about the possible lawsuit that loomed large if someone didn't understand kidney transplantation and fired John. I also doubted that Penn would want to take a chance on John in Cannes. Stopping the flow of gossip at its source was a sore spot between us for a few days. I finally gave up on trying to persuade John to try to quell the gossip when one of my sage friends suggested that attempting to stop the gossip might make the story even more alluring to the gossiper.

Five weeks after the surgery and after weeks of not getting along, I decided to ask John directly what the problem was. I did this during our first excursion to a movie theater after our operations, just as the film was about to start. "Why are you so angry at me?

"I'm not angry at you. You are angry at me because I put you through so much pain and suffering."

I let John's answer sink in for a while, all the way through Woody Allen's *Sweet and Lowdown*. When the movie was over and we were walking home, I realized that John was feeling guilty for all of the pain he had put me through and the pain and suffering he thought I still felt. I told John that the truth was, I didn't experience pain any more, and I guess for the same reason that the pain of childbirth is quickly forgotten, I could hardly remember the pain that I had felt. "John, maybe you feel guilty and that is why you've been so hostile to me."

"That's a possibility,." John admitted.

And then, just like that, he went back to being his sweetest self.

For the few weeks before his admission of guilt, while suffering through his standoffishness and indifference, I had thought that he had only been nice to me in the weeks before the surgery just to get my kidney. I had felt so used and angry. I had told him how I felt on numerous occasions and he had denied that he was being nasty to me. My question—posed at just the time he was ready to answer—was an epiphany for both of us that helped us turn the corner back to some degree of emotional normalcy. I no longer wondered if a Nobel Prize winner would have been the appropriate recipient for my kidney. I had given my kidney to just the right person. My kidney had gone to the man I love.

The day after our movie excursion I felt exhausted. I thought that I would spend another day lying around and reading the paper. Then I decided to get up and start moving around on the theory that I might feel better. I decided to pursue the activity that for me was the most therapeutic—shopping. It was one of the activities that I thought might be lost to me forever because of some dire complication from the surgery. I decided first to brave my favorite store, the discount department store Ross, and then to visit Strawbridge and Clothier, one of a dying breed of Philadelphia department stores. We needed a lightweight vacuum cleaner. I spent a few hours browsing in Ross and then turned to the more serious vacuum cleaner shopping in Strawbridge's. I found the perfect vacuum cleaner. I carried the lightweight machine down to a cab. I felt independent again, like myself. It had been less than six weeks since the operation. I was almost completely recovered. Then I came home, did the laundry, made dinner, emptied the dishwasher and changed the kitty litter. The next day I paid for doing so much. I didn't care. I knew that I could do everything myself again.

I realized that it was finally time for us to call Brent to see how he was doing after donating a kidney to his brother. I felt sufficiently recovered that nothing he could say would bother me. John called him and reported on the conversation. "He is still having trouble getting up from the sofa but he feels like he is on the mend." I realized that I had made the right decision in not calling Brent soon after his surgery, the one with the gigantic incision. It might have made me lose my nerve, even though I knew that an open procedure was just a long shot for me. It had been more than eight weeks after Brent's surgery and he was still incapacitated. I had had surgery weeks after he did, and I was back to work and almost back to my usual routine. I realized what a boon the development of the closed procedure had been to live organ donation. I was still not convinced that I would have given John my kidney had the open procedure been my only alternative.

Just when both of us were getting back to our usual routines, John woke up in the middle of the night, drenched in sweat. He had a sore throat and was coughing. He panicked. He thought that he had some dreaded infection that his body wouldn't be able to fight off because of the immunosuppressants. I calmed him down and put on a vaporizer. It worked. Our first bout with an imagined infection was over. We soon learned that sometimes a cold is just a cold. Although colds can last somewhat longer in someone who is taking immunosuppressants, they usually go away relatively quickly.

Always looming over our heads in the six weeks after the surgery was the threat of rejection. John's creatinine in the last few weeks had gone from 1.3 to 1.4 to 1.5, my lay idea of creeping up. I hadn't told John about Dr. Grossman's telling me about that kind of rejection. I just worried to myself that that might be what we were facing. John had to miss a blood test because there was a foot of snow. I hoped that the snow would melt soon and I redoubled my kidney's boxing to kill the cells that shouldn't be there. The other thing that I worried about was that John had been on high doses of immunosuppressants for a long time. Often after a few weeks the dosages would be lowered. Because of his rejection episode, the doses remained high. The higher the dose of immunosuppressants, the less chance of rejection. The higher the dose of immunosuppressants, the greater the possibility of infection and drug side effects. Each time someone near us coughed or sneezed, John flinched. So did I.

A few days after the foot-high snow John went for a blood test. We didn't get the results immediately because Dr. Grossman was on vacation. The night before John was scheduled to see Dr. Grossman and get the results of his blood test, John realized that he had urinated very infrequently, yet another possible sign of rejection in the manual. I again started my imaginary pounding on the cells I thought were trying to invade Sydney Joan Kidney. When John saw Dr. Grossman, his creatinine was 1.4. We were on the right track. The creatinine wasn't creeping up anymore. A fluctuation between 1.3 and 1.5 we would take. Dr. Grossman lowered one of the immunosuppressants. John could wait two weeks before getting another blood test. I felt as though we might be getting out of the woods. Something I read said that the first eight weeks after transplant are critical. Most problems rear their heads during those two months. We were almost there.

Two weeks later John e-mailed Dr. Grossman for his most recent blood test results. His creatinine was 1.3. Mine was 1.2. Now that John seemed all right, I started to worry about myself. I had been feeling a pain in the area of my right kidney. It could have been low back pain or there could be something wrong with my only kidney. I convinced myself that nothing was really wrong. I laid it to hyper anxiety about that kidney and the return of adolescent hypochondria, both of which I would have to learn to live with. The pain lessened and went away.

SYDNEY JOAN KIDNEY
AND JULIETTE AT TWO MONTHS

It was mid-February, two months after the transplant, and we were expecting visitors. Very special visitors. Isabelle, Didier and their two-month-old daughter, Juliette. Juliette was born not only on the same day John had the transplant, but at about the same time, even accounting for the five-hour time difference between Paris and Philadelphia. Isabelle had had a difficult delivery. We were having a rough time at just about the same time of day. Isabelle's and our rough periods both resulted in new life. We were very eager to meet the new baby. We felt a real bond with her even before we met. What were the odds that our transplant and her birth would be at the same time on the same day?

We picked up our French friends at Philadelphia International Airport. They had flown on American Airlines by way of New York. It was before Air France, Isabelle and Didier's preferred carrier, had its nonstop Paris-to-Philadelphia flight.

The little family arrived at the airport exhausted. The American Airlines flight attendants paid almost no attention to the baby, something Isabelle said would never have happened had they flown Air France. The only amenity that American had given to the Alfandarys was a cardboard box for Juliette to sleep in, and the airline warned our friends that they had to keep the box because there would not be another one forthcoming for the flight home.

Juliette was a real beauty. She had chubby cheeks, lovely green eyes and light hair. She was a sweet baby who, even after her long plane trip, was agreeable and smiling.

When Isabelle, Didier and Juliette arrived at our house we had three cats, Cinder, Ella and Mickey. Mickey had been suffering the ravages of thyroid disease and he looked a little like a skeleton with fur, but he remained a kindly old man. When Mickey didn't have much of an appetite and was quite lethargic,. John suggested to the vet that maybe steroids would work to give Mickey more of an appetite. They had certainly worked as appetite enhancers for John. And so Mickey wound up on prednisone too, and for a while they both ate everything in sight. We didn't know it before Isabelle arrived, but there was no love lost between her and cats in general. Cinder and Ella weren't much of a problem because they pretty much kept to themselves. Mickey, though, was like a dog. He loved people and attention and had no pride in attempting to get the attention he craved. Like most cats, he had a second sense about people who were allergic, or who plain didn't like cats, and he made it his business to pay attention to them in an effort to change their minds. He made a beeline for Isabelle and curled up in her lap.

About a half-hour after Isabelle, Didier, Juliette and their luggage, including the American Airlines white box cum crib, arrived in the living room, Mickey had begun to lick them all, much to Isabelle's consternation. After being told "no," "no," and "no" and "down, Mickey," he persevered. His crowning blow was to walk over to the airline box, sniff it carefully and then start to squat over it. Didier stopped Mickey in mid-squat. To Mickey the airline box was not a crib, but a box just like the one he had in the basement. By the time the Alfandarys left, Mickey had made Isabelle a cat lover. She never forgot to ask about him.

While Isabelle and Didier were visiting us, we told them that John had many questions that no one was willing to answer definitively. At bottom, John wanted to be reassured unequivocally that everything would be all right. Try to get an assurance like that out of an American doctor, even doctors like the really good ones John had at Penn. You really couldn't blame them since a raft of malpractice suits has caused them to constantly be looking over their shoulders to see when the next lawsuit would be coming around the corner. I knew that John would be the last person anyone would reassure since he announced to everyone who treated him that I was a medical malpractice lawyer.

Didier was amazed that no one would definitively answer all of John's questions and was chagrined that no one would assure John that everything would be all right. Didier told us that in France the doctors were considered to be descended from the priest class and that they ministered to both the body and the soul. As Isabelle described it, the priests were at one time the doctors in France, and bedside manner and taking time with the patient to allay fears had always been and continued to be an important part of practicing medicine. That priestly approach to the whole patient has in this country been buried under a tangle of HMOs and PPOs. No doctor here has the time to minister to the whole patient. Of course, there are virtually no malpractice cases in France, so doctors there can take a risk and minister to souls too. HMOs and the economics of American medicine do not allow doctors enough time to minister even to the bodies of their patients, let alone their minds and souls. They have too many patients to see and are too mired in paperwork.

Isabelle and Didier hatched a plan to reassure John. They asked him to write out all of his questions and fax them to Isabelle's father, Emanuel Weitzenblum, a professor of pulmonology in Strasbourg. Dr. Weitzenblum would relay the questions to his colleague and friend who ran the transplant service there so that John could get the answers he sought.

John relaxed for the first time since the transplant when the answers to his questions arrived from France. In a nutshell, the French transplant specialist said that the worst was likely over and that John would probably be fine. Of course, she didn't have to worry about getting sued by the patient's wife if she was wrong.

Isabelle confided to us that when she first told her father that John was having a transplant that he too was concerned. He was only worried because he thought that John was having a lung transplant, a much more involved and dangerous procedure. When Dr. Weitzenblum found out it was "only a kidney transplant," he couldn't figure out why Isabelle or we would be worried at all.

We had all of the benefits of the best of American medicine when it came to the transplant itself. For follow-up, we had both American medicine and the assurances of the priestly French medical establishment.

Before Isabelle, Didier and tiny Juliette left Philadelphia, a city they loved because they thought it was so European, we took them to a very special luncheon sponsored by a host of donor organizations. The lunch was to thank live organ donors. I wanted to go to the luncheon, although I wasn't sure why. Surely, John's getting steadily better should have been enough thanks for me. I guess that his recovery and the Elsa Peretti bean weren't enough. I felt so proud of what I had done that I wanted to share my pride with Billie, Maureen, Bonnie, Isabelle and Didier, the friends who had helped us through it, and with Juliette, who had been born at precisely the same moment that John's life started over again, when Sydney Joan Kidney moved from my body to his.

Many of my friends were at the luncheon. Even Juliette was there, although she slept through the whole thing and if you asked her now, she wouldn't remember anything about it. The room where the luncheon was held was decorated with a gaggle of heart-shaped red and white balloons. It was the day before Valentine's Day. Each table had a gigantic Hershey's Kiss festooned with flowers. The chocoholic in me loved that. There were ninety-eight donors of kidneys and livers, people who had donated their own organs or parts of them to their mothers, fathers, sisters, brothers, children, wives, husbands or close friends. Many of the recipients who came to honor their donors were small children. One child received a piece of his father's liver and in turn donated his own tiny liver, which was being rejected by his own body, to another small child. The donors and recipients were from every racial and religious group, all sharing the common experience of giving and receiving.

An assistant to the U.S. Surgeon General presented the donor pins. When my name was called, he greeted me with a warm smile, and handed me a donor pin and a certificate. "Who did you donate to?" I heard John and my friends clapping and cheering in the background.

I smiled broadly and said, "My husband."

The camera shutters clicked. There was more applause and cheering. My fifteen minutes of fame, as promised by Andy Warhol, was only about three minutes, but what a great three minutes it was.

My pain had completely subsided. The scars were healing. My abdomen was again symmetrical. A two-piece bathing suit was no longer out of the question. I had had my final appointment with Dr. Naji. John was feeling better. His kidney function was stable. It had all—all of it, from that first meeting in Montreal to the donor luncheon—been worth it.

Lightning Source UK Ltd.
Milton Keynes UK
UKHW04f0610160718
325764UK00001B/64/P